CHILDREN
PRAYING

CHILDREN PRAYING

Why and

How to Pray

With Your Children

JOAN BEL GEDDES

SORIN BOOKS   Notre Dame, IN

International Standard Book Number: 1-893732-04-5
Library of Congress Catalog Card Number: 99-61899
Cover design: Cynthia Dunne
Text design: Brian C. Conley
Printed and bound in the United States of America.

To my three beloved children,
Anne, Nicholas, and Katie,
who taught me so much
about what life and love are all about

CONTENTS

ACKNOWLEDGMENTS

I owe a lifetime of thanks to the many writers quoted in this book. They come from all continents and many centuries, and their accumulated wisdom has not only helped me for many years but provided the idea to produce this book.

I also wish to thank personal friends, particularly Noreen Drukker, and Alice Bates, John Catoir, Joe and Sally Cunneen, José and Catherine De Vinck, Dorothy Fabian, Margaret Kahn, Michael Leach, John and Marilee Reiner, Mark Stern, and Barry Ulanov, all of whom encouraged my interest in writing about children and religion.

And I owe most particular thanks to my editors John J. Kirvan and Julie Hahnenberg and to Frank J. Cunningham, publisher of Sorin Books; it was their enthusiasm for this project that made it evolve from a dream into a reality.

Introduction

THOUGHTS ABOUT
CHILDREN AND PRAYER

"There are as many ways to pray as there are moments in life. Sometimes we seek out a quiet spot and want to be alone, sometimes we look for a friend and want to be together. Sometimes we like a book, sometimes we prefer music. Sometimes we want to sing out with hundreds, sometimes only whisper with a few. Sometimes we want to say it with words, sometimes with a deep silence."

—Henri Nouwen,
in *With Open Hands*

Once upon a time, the normal and formal way to begin and end a child's day was with morning and bedtime prayers. All "good" and "well brought up" children got down on their knees and recited out loud a set of traditional phrases, usually beginning or ending with requests for God to bless their families and friends and neighbors, wishing everyone well. The children were learning, or trying to learn, to love people, not to hate or hurt them.

Today, however, in most American homes, such prayers have lost favor. Some parents still encourage them

*"How should we pray? ...
We can talk to God with
the same intimacy and
confidence and trust as a
little child talks to his
father. ... We do not need
to talk to God in any special
kind of religious or theological language. ... We do not
need to talk to God in any
special position. Kneeling,
standing, sitting, lying, it is
all the same. As a child runs
to his father and tells him
everything in the days when
he is very young and very
innocent and very trusting,
so we can talk to God. ...
We must once and for all get
rid of the idea that prayer is
something stilted and unnat-
ural. It is the most natural
thing in the world ... a child
talking to his father. ..."*

—William Barclay,
in *A Guide to
Daily Prayer*

while their children are very small,
but both youngsters and parents are
apt to lose interest fairly soon, and
even give them up entirely. The busy
and stressful pace of today's family
life doesn't seem to lend itself to
such prayer activity, and our secular-
ized society offers little or no encour-
agement to it.

But praying with our children
can have great psychological as well
as spiritual value. Both psychology
and religion are concerned with the
soul, the intellect, and emotions, and
with how these affect behavior. The
main difference is vocabulary—what
psychologists might call "negative
thinking" or "positive thinking" religion would call "sins" or "virtues."
If children are exposed early enough
to "good" (i.e., "healthy") thoughts
and attitudes, they may be able to
avoid going through experiences that
produce their opposites. By emphasizing through prayer such qualities
as confidence, optimism, and generosity (i.e., faith, hope, and love),
their souls will expand beyond self-
centeredness and open up to a reliable source of strength.

Both morning and bedtime
prayers are healthful habits, just as
brushing our teeth, taking a bath, or
taking vitamins each day is, and for
the same reasons: they help us to
keep clean, they get rid of that which

might hurt us, and they strengthen us. Bedtime prayers are particularly useful because they can serve as a sturdy bridge that carries a child from activity to repose, from excitement to calm, providing a way to become tranquil before falling asleep, thus encouraging pleasant dreams. They can also help to build a warm rapport between parents and children. And, most important of all, they can be a means of opening and expanding a child's heart and mind and spiritual horizon wholesomely, happily, and helpfully. By taking a few minutes each day to think of and pray for the welfare of other people, a child forms the habit of being generous and loving.

"Everyone prays in their own language, and there is no language that God does not understand."

—Duke Ellington

"Prayer, it seems to me, is one of the simplest necessities of life, as basic to the individual as sunshine, food and water—and at times, of course, more so."

—Dwight D. Eisenhower

WHY DO SO MANY CHILDREN (AND OTHER PEOPLE) STOP PRAYING?

There are, of course, many reasons that children and others stop praying. If you have stopped, or have let your children stop, you already know some of them. Two of the main reasons are fairly obvious: (1) you have decided that prayer doesn't really do any good, or (2) you aren't really sure whether it does any good or not, but you haven't personally found it helpful, meaningful, or interesting, so perhaps it's a waste of time.

Some parents give up saying morning and evening prayers with their children (as well as grace at meals) because they become discouraged and distressed at their children's lack of comprehension and interest. Many children do tend to wriggle and giggle and fidget during prayers, and pious parents, deeply offended, may decide it would be better to say no prayers at all than to allow them to be said irreverently. They may get annoyed at their children's lack of seriousness and concentration and their short attention span, and prayer time may turn into scolding time. Then the children may begin to dislike praying, and the time that was meant to be marked by sweet serenity and love becomes instead an occasion for family battles.

If prayers seem meaningless (hence dull) or become the cause of arguments (hence irritating) it isn't at all surprising that children can hardly wait for them to end. And once their parents stop supervising them, these children promptly stop praying, which is one more reason parents decide to give up on trying to teach their children to pray—why insist on a habit that you know is going to be abandoned the minute you stop insisting on it? So who can blame them for deciding it would be better to say no prayers at all than to pursue a time-consuming habit that seems to contribute nothing important to their children's moral, emotional, or spiritual health?

But most parents want to help their children learn to be good people, and I suspect that most of them, even if their own faith is quite weak, wish they could give their children some faith—so they do try to for a while. They plod along, trying to be patient, wishing they knew how to make prayer attractive to their youngsters although they themselves may have always thought of prayer as a duty, not a pleasure. How can you communicate a skill which you yourself don't have?

But believe it or not, even people who are not religious can benefit from prayer. Even if they think they are just talking to themselves, that nobody powerful and loving is listening to them, pausing at times to listen to their own deepest thoughts, to wish other people well, and to express appreciation for their blessings, to make good resolutions, and to review the day's accomplishments and failures can be—as Anne Frank realized over fifty years ago—peace-giving and strengthening. In her famous diary she wrote:

> People who have a religion should be glad, for not everyone has the gift of believing in heavenly things. You don't necessarily even have to be afraid of punishment after death; purgatory, hell and heaven are things that a lot of people can't accept, but still a religion, it doesn't matter which, keeps a person on the right path. It isn't the fear of God but the upholding of one's honor and conscience. How noble and good everyone could be if, every evening before falling asleep, they were to recall to their minds the events of the whole day and consider exactly what has been good and bad. Then, without realizing it, you try to improve yourself at the start of each new day; of course, you achieve quite a lot in the course of time. Anyone can do this, it costs nothing and is certainly very helpful. Whoever doesn't know it must learn and find by experience that "a quiet conscience makes one strong."

I have a friend who strongly believes in the power of prayer even though he is not sure that he believes in a personal God. When he was growing up, he and his four brothers used to gather around their parents for family prayers each day, and he says that "this gave us a time every day when all fights stopped, all pandemonium was interrupted, all problems were suspended, all tensions relaxed. And as a family it gave us a tremendous peace and solidarity

"More things are wrought by prayer than this world dreams of."

—Alfred, Lord Tennyson

and strength and security that I really don't think could have been acquired in any other way."

For people who do believe in a personal God, prayer is, obviously, even more important because it is utterly illogical, even insulting, to say we "believe in" and "love" someone and yet never speak to him. What would you think of someone who claimed to love you but who never wanted to contact you?

HOW NOT TO PRAY—USING PREFABRICATED PRAYERS

When we don't really know how to pray, we tend to rely on prayers that other people have composed. It seems easiest to try to make our children memorize formulas, but often these prayers are in a several-hundred-year-old vocabulary that the children don't understand. They become small robots, dutifully repeating phrases that have only a slight relationship to their own private thoughts. Words they utter that have no real meaning for them are confusing rather than inspiring.

Sometimes the results are comical. (We should remember, of course, that if we laugh at their mistakes we may embarrass the children and make them reluctant to have anything more to do with religion.) I remember a girl who thought the Negro spiritual "There Is a Balm in Gilead" meant there was a *bomb* there, and she couldn't figure out why that was supposed to be comforting. There was also the young son of a friend of mine who came home from kindergarten one day after a Christmas pageant, which included a carol about being grouped around the young Virgin, and he asked his mother, "What's a round young virgin?" And then there are Catholic children who, when going to confession, say, "I am hardly sorry," instead of, "I am heartily sorry."

Speaking of being heartily sorry, I will never forget the night when I learned how important it is not to have a child always rely on memorized prayers. My young daughter Anne was upset because, she told me, she had been very naughty that day. I suggested, "Then make an act of contrition"—a prayer of repentance that some young children are asked to memorize. She screwed up her face and concentrated hard but then wailed in a panic, "I don't remember how it goes!" Thus a once-memorized verbal formula meant to express repentance had taken the place of what it was meant to convey. All she needed to do to relieve herself of guilt was to actually be contrite, as she was, and say (and mean it) that she was extremely sorry for what she had done and wouldn't do it again.

Another possible problem with using traditional prayers with children is that although they often express beautiful thoughts in mellifluous phrases, they are apt to have only slight relevance to youngsters. They were undoubtedly extremely sincere and meaningful to the devout saints or eloquent poets who composed them, but they frequently express a passionate degree of faith and a fervor that so far exceeds what the average child feels that they might seem puzzling, even unbelievable. This difficulty could apply to adults too, except that we've had enough experience of the world to be able to recognize and admire geniuses, whether in the arts or sciences or spiritual life, without feeling ashamed that we are not among them.

Still one more problem with traditional prayers is that some of them are theologically complicated—it's not only the language that is beyond young children's comprehension but the beliefs they express. Some others go to the opposite extreme and are oversimplified, insipid, bland, and saccharine. Repeating banal phrases over and over again is why so many people find prayer boring.

However, this does not demonstrate that *prayer* is boring but rather that the *way* in which we are praying is boring. If we pray mechanically, routinely, superficially, or monotonously, we are bound to be bored. We have turned what is meant to be a help to us into an irksome chore.

Whether prefabricated prayers are eloquent or trite, they usually reach children's ears but not always their hearts or brains. Prayer should be at the level where a person really is. As the Quakers say, it must "speak to our condition" if it is not going to be irrelevant and useless. So instead of having children listen to and mouth words someone else has composed, children should be shown how to do their own praying, how to reach way down inside themselves and way out beyond themselves so that they can increase their understanding of themselves, of other people, and of the whole world.

Their ability to do this will of course vary from child to child and from age to age. A preschooler cannot be expected to be as fluent in expressing his or her deepest thoughts as a sixth-grader. Nor will the thoughts be as complex. So in teaching children to pray we must take into consideration the different stages of child development:

1 — Intra-Uterine (the period before birth)
2 — Neonatal (the first 4 weeks of life)
3 — Infancy (the first 2 years of life)
4 — Preschool years (usually from 2 to 5 years)
5 — Elementary school years (from 5 to 10 or 12)
6 — Prepubescence (in girls 10-12; in boys 12-14)
7 — Adolescence (in girls 12-18; in boys 14-20)

This is the sequence of stages through which children's development takes place, although the specific ages at which each stage occurs will vary from child to child. Some youngsters are precocious; others are late bloomers.

Einstein's parents actually were afraid this genius was retarded because he didn't learn to talk until he was five years old. But as someone (I forget who) wisely said, parents of slow learners should not worry because they may know a lot about raspberries but know nothing about grapes.

Praying with your children will help you get to know them well. Don't try to push them and increase their faith too rapidly, or hold them back either. As they progress from stage to stage their questions and comments will guide you.

As children grow older you may even discover that in spite of my warnings about "prefabricated" prayers some children may come across prayers that really appeal to them, prayers that in fact do "speak to their condition," and they may actually want to memorize them. In that case, when the choice is theirs, don't discourage them from using them, as long as they supplement instead of replace their own individual praying. When they grow still older, they may recall such memorized prayers from their childhood with great affection, like old friends.

ANOTHER WAY NOT TO PRAY—PUTTING YOUR OWN WORDS IN YOUR CHILD'S MOUTH

Some ambitious parents try to escape from the drawbacks of using time-honored but uninspiring prayers by being personally creative. They improvise and invent new personal prayers for their children to say in the children's own vocabulary, at the children's own mental level. They sincerely and imaginatively and empathetically try to make the ideas relevant—and sometimes they succeed.

But even those who manage to compose attractive and relevant new prayers may end up, in actuality, praying for and by themselves. Their children may listen to what they say and repeat it, like parrots, but the words and ideas might not really do the trick. And as the children get older they are apt to resent having their parents put words in their mouths—or, on the other hand, they may come to rely so much on their well-meaning, inventive, and articulate parents to do their thinking and verbalizing for them that they never get around to learning how to think for themselves or how to express their own thoughts.

We should never try to impose any set of ideas or attitudes on someone who doesn't really fully understand or agree with them, or encourage someone to pretend to accept them. When we do this—no matter how well motivated—it is more apt to produce mindless sheep than intelligent, strong, vigorous, loving people (which is what real prayer should do). At its very best, repeating prayers invented by someone else—even by a loving and understanding parent—tends to simulate rather than stimulate devotion.

So How Should We Go About Teaching Children to Pray?

We must realize, and help our children realize, that the best prayer is meant to be a real conversation between us and God. Genuine prayer should be a two-way street with us talking to God and God talking to us. It should not be a continual stream of words, of petitions or apologies. Listening is as important a part of any conversation as talking is, and silent prayer is as important as verbal prayer. We need silence in which to think, silence in which to reflect, silence in which to wait, and silence in which to listen.

To listen to what?

Joan of Arc was sneered at when she said she heard voices when she prayed. Her hostile, skeptical judges asked her, "What makes you think you're so special that saints and angels would speak to you when they don't to other people?" She is said to have replied, "Oh, they do speak to other people—but most people don't listen."

Explain to your children that God is their True Friend who made them and loves them, and that they can talk to him whenever they like, even though they can't see him. (Once a friend of mine who was a school teacher criticized me for talking to my daughter who was in kindergarten about God at an age when, she said, no child was old enough to be able to comprehend the concept of God, and to prove this she asked Anne, "How do you know there's a God or what he's like if there is one, since you can't see him?" Without any prompting, Anne stared at her with pity, as if she were lacking some marbles, and said, "Well, of course you can't see him because God is Love, and love is invisible, but you know perfectly well it exists, don't you?")

Without guidance, however, silence during prayer may trouble children. They may ask God lots of questions and then get puzzled and upset when all they receive in reply is silence, and they may even decide he's not real after all. But there is a lovely little Jewish saying that may reassure them: "I believe in the sun even when it is not shining; I believe in love even when it is absent; I believe in God even when He is silent."

We should explain that even when it seems to them that God is silent, he never really deserts us. It's just that he doesn't speak in a human voice or vocabulary. But God does truly speak to us (in what theologians call "creative words") by putting good thoughts into our heads. His Spirit enters us when we open our minds and hearts to him, freely and with love (and our minds and hearts are like parachutes—they only function properly when they are open).

Rabbi Marc Gellman and Monsignor Thomas Hartman, in a delightful book they wrote together for children called *How Do You Spell God?*, have described how God speaks to us:

> Talking is not nearly as important as listening. When you talk all you hear is your own voice. When you listen, you may hear something that can make you wise. All religions teach us to listen. ... It is not that hard to hear God; it is just hard to believe that what you are hearing really is from God. We hear God when that voice inside of us says "Don't punch Herbie in the nose!" That inside voice is called our conscience, but it is really the voice of God speaking to us to help us be better people.

Even though children may begin to realize that God does speak to them, there will be some times when they may not like what he tells them. Why?

WHAT PRAYER CANNOT DO FOR US OR OUR CHILDREN

God is our Creator and our guide, but not a rabbit's foot or a carnival magician or an indulgent grandmother who will give us anything we want. And he is infinitely wiser than we are, so we should not be surprised if he doesn't always take our advice or respect our wishes. It is both silly and futile to think we can somehow cajole, bribe, bargain with, or force the Almighty to fulfill our every wish.

"God gave us two ears and one mouth, to show us that we should listen twice as much as we speak."

—Arab Proverb

"God is perfect love and perfect wisdom. We do not pray in order to change His will, but to bring our wills in harmony with His."

—William Temple

A child may pray for good weather when planning a picnic and be crushed when it rains instead. But a local farmer may be praying for rain on that same day, rain he needs for his crops, and the child isn't, after all, the only person God is looking out for. As an Irish saying explains, "It's harder than you think to run the world."

Children should not be encouraged to pray in such a way that if their prayers are not "answered" they will feel disillusioned. Disappointed, yes, of course, but not indignant. Explain that this doesn't mean God doesn't love them and want them to be happy, any more than you stop loving them when you sometimes have to deny them something they want.

They should pray honestly, with hope, but not with a superstitious overconfidence, nor with a feeling that they know better than God does what they should have at any given time.

What Prayer Can Do for Us and Our Children

Although God does not always give us everything we want, he can and does help us clarify our thinking, strengthen our good resolutions, and increase our ability to love—and love

"Lord, You know what is best for me.
Let this or that be done as You please.
Give what You will,
How much You will,
And when You will."

—Thomas à Kempis

"You cannot read the Gospels without seeing that Jesus did not tell men how to be good in the manner of the moralists of every age, he told them how to be happy."

—Sir Thomas Taylor

"Do you want to know one of the best ways to win over people and lead them to God? It consists in giving them joy and making them happy."

—Saint Francis of Assisi

is something unique in that when we give it away we don't lose it. In fact, the more love we give others the more we will ourselves be filled with love—a paradox that is a beautiful confirmation of what Saint Francis of Assisi said about how "it is in giving [not in getting] that we receive."

Children must be taught to be utterly truthful when they pray, instead of trying to impress God, themselves, and us by showing off and pretending to seem holier than they really feel. So they needn't be afraid to tell God how disappointed they are, when they are, or even to admit that they are sometimes very angry with him. He knows our thoughts already anyway, so you can assure them that he won't be shocked!

If we teach our children to avoid all affectations when they pray, they will acquire mental, emotional, and spiritual health. And we will have given our children a gift far more valuable than toys or jewels, a solid rock on which they can stand all their lives with confidence, no matter what violent storms attack them now or later in life. We will have taught them a reliable technique for coping with both little and large problems. We will also have shown them a way to acknowledge privileges and joys with intense appreciation, and a way to examine their personal goals and values thoughtfully and creatively. We will have given them both roots and wings. Prayer can accomplish all these things if one prays "in spirit and truth," not just with one's lips.

> *"People go to a football game today and shout their heads off, or go to a circus and cheer act after act. They become enthusiastic about everything conceivable, but when it comes to spiritual matters they think we are supposed to become sober and wear black, and never have a good time or enjoy a religious event."*
>
> —Billy Graham

> *"These things I have spoken to you that my joy may be in you, and your joy may be full."*
>
> —John 15:11

HOW CAN WE HELP CHILDREN ACTUALLY ENJOY PRAYER?

A quick but heartfelt morning prayer can be as happiness-producing as a delicious breakfast. It helps to get each new day off to a fine start by putting a child in a happy mood prepared to face with confidence whatever will come up.

And bedtime prayers can be as much looked forward to as a nightly bedtime story. They should be approached as a privilege, an opportunity, not as a dry duty. They give children a chance to do many useful and comforting things: to recall happy experiences and thus prolong them; to sort out and examine their most perplexing thoughts, and unsnarl confusion; to release private fears and worries and thus get rid of them; to face their defects and defeats calmly with courage and to learn from them.

Young children love ceremonies and are comforted by routines that are predictable and reliable. Routine gives them a sense of stability and security. And they enjoy rituals. Just watch youngsters as they carefully, solemnly, arrange their bath toys, or listen to them when they sternly correct you if you omit some minor detail in a favorite story, or if you make an unexpected change in bathtime or bedtime procedures. If their toys are not placed near or on their beds

> *"Christ came to bring joy: joy to children, joy to parents, joy to families and to friends, joy to workers and to scholars, joy to the sick and joy to the elderly, joy to all humanity. In a true sense, joy is the keynote of the Christian message and the recurring motif of the Gospels. Be messengers of joy."*
>
> —Pope John Paul II

> *"How necessary it is to cultivate a spirit of joy. To act lovingly is to begin to feel loving, and certainly to act joyfully brings joy to others, which in turn makes one feel joyful. I believe we are called to the duty of delight."*
>
> —Dorothy Day

just so and the light is or is not turned off just before or just after you have said whatever is your usual form of goodnight, and if you don't hug them just before or right after tucking them into their covers, most little children will go into a rage or a panic—which is why so many problems occur when new babysitters don't do things in exactly the "right" way.

This enjoyment of ritual comes in handy when you begin taking your children to church. Don't expect most of them, at least at first, to sit quietly through long services and what are to them unintelligible sermons, but on days when there will be processions and other special ceremonies, they will love to watch or participate. (See Part Five.)

All prayers—morning, afternoon, and evening, impromptu or as part of religious ceremonies—are important as long as they are conducive to joy. As Saint Teresa of Avila once said: "From somber, serious, sullen saints deliver us, O Lord!"

Thomas More and Martin Luther disagreed about many things, but there was one thing they both believed: that cheerfulness and a sense of humor are important.

In one of his prayers, More asked,

"Therefore, whatever is just, whatever is pure, whatever is pleasing, whatever is commendable, if there is any excellence, and if there is anything worthy of praise, think about these things ... and the God of peace will be with you."

—Philippians 4:8, 9

Give me, Lord, a soul that knows nothing of boredom, groans and sighs. Never let me be overly concerned for this inconstant thing I call me. Lord, give me a sense of humor so that I may take some happiness from this life and share it with others.

And Luther felt so strongly about the value of fun and a sense of humor that he once wrote: "If you're not allowed to laugh in heaven, then I don't want to go there."

Both of them must also have agreed with the following diagnosis: "A glad heart makes for good health" (Proverbs 17:22).

So keep your children's prayer life focused on joy, not exclusively on woes and sins. Sins are something to get rid of whereas happiness is something to treasure and hold on to tightly. If prayer doesn't make children happy, I would rather none of them ever prayed, except that I truly think it is impossible to be as happy as possible without the comfort and inspiration provided by faith and prayer.

Once you have taught your children why and how to enjoy prayer there will be a wonderful bonus for you: you will not only have developed a happier and more loving and stronger relationship with your children, but at the same time you will inevitably have taught yourself how to enjoy prayer more.

On the following pages there are suggestions for many different types of children's prayers. Part One discusses daily prayers, those in the mornings and at mealtimes, and Part Two looks at evening prayers. To quote Rabbi Gellman and Monsignor Hartman once again:

> Some of the prayers you say to God have never been said before by anyone. These are personal prayers. Personal prayers come from your soul, hit your lips on the way out, and go straight on to God ... All human beings need to say four things in their lives. The four things that all

"There is no beautifier of complexion, or form, or behavior, like the wish to scatter joy—and not pain—around us."

—Ralph Waldo Emerson

"Joy is the most infallible sign of the presence of God."

—Teilhard de Chardin

people need to say are: Thanks! Wow! Gimme! and Ooops!

So the section on evening prayers that follows in this book includes a "Thank You" part (Thanks and Wow), a "Sorry" part (Oops), and a "Please Help" and "God Bless" part (Gimme). In addition, there are suggestions for how to use prayer in unexpected situations, as well as descriptions of some special celebrations to which children can look forward throughout the year. Sprinkled among my own comments and suggestions you will continue to find many pertinent quotations from other people whose words I have found helpful in raising my own children, and which I hope you too will find interesting and inspiring.

Part One

DAILY PRAYERS: MORNINGS AND MEALTIMES

"Now before I run to play,
Let me not forget to pray
To God Who kept me through the night
And waked me with the morning light.
Help me, God, to love Thee more
Than I have ever loved before.
In my work and in my play,
Be Thou with me through the day.
Amen."

—Traditional morning prayer

"In the morning, when I say my prayers, thou wilt hear me."

—Psalm 5:3

"Thank you, God, for the day that is beginning now. Help me make it the important and wonderful day it can be. Help me live it so that the world will be better because I lived in it today. All day long, help me bring happiness and love to everyone I meet."

—Morning prayer, author unknown

"Lord, I expect to be very busy today; If I forget Thee, do not Thou forget me."

—Anonymous

Childhood is the beginning, the morning, of life, a brand new creation, like a new day full of possibilities that are not yet known. That is why taking good care of our young children is such an important and sacred responsibility. How a child will develop, for good or ill, depends on many factors beyond our control, but in the early years the most influential one by far is the child's parents. And each new day, like each child, is a valuable gift, not to be neglected or taken for granted, but cherished.

How soon should we start introducing children to God? The question is in a way meaningless because God has been in intimate contact with them ever since they were conceived. Recent research in child development has given us new knowledge about how much children have learned from their infinitely skillful Teacher even while they were still in the womb and how quickly most of them continue to learn after emerging from there. Think how much they already know when they are born: how to reach for and swallow food, how to refresh themselves through sleep, how to express their needs and ask for help by crying, and even how to recognize their mother's voice.

Some parents believe that singing and talking and even reading aloud to a child while it is still in the womb gets it off to a head start in life, and most parents realize instinctively that singing and talking to their newborn babies, as well as rocking and hugging and providing other stimulation, accelerates their learning as well as making them happy.

During the first year of life it has been said that children study harder and learn more than they ever will during four years of college. One of the thousands of things that lucky infants soon learn is that when they cry a loving person quickly responds, and this teaches them trust and gratitude. They also very soon learn to play, at first with their thumbs, then their toes, and then with other toys. In the past some people discouraged child's play because they had such a grim and earnest notion of virtue that they considered play frivolous. But children learn a great deal through playing, without knowing they are learning anything.

Why did Jesus say that unless we all become like little children we will not be able to enter the kingdom of heaven? For centuries many theologians, apparently forgetting or ignoring Jesus' love for all children, thought that infants were so polluted by original sin that they couldn't go to heaven if they died before they were baptized. Today almost nobody believes such nonsense, but we are very much aware of babies' *un*original sins. Though cute, they are self-centered and greedy (except for one astonishing newborn named Nicholas who,

> *"God, my Father, thank you for giving me my life and this new day. God, the Holy Spirit, thank you for helping me learn how to be good. Dear Jesus, help me love you with all my heart and with all my soul and with all my mind, and to love my neighbors, my brothers and sisters all over the world, as you do."*
>
> —Prayer to the Blessed Trinity

> *"Play is the highest form of research."*
>
> —Albert Einstein

31

> *"It is requisite for the relaxation of the mind that we make use, from time to time, of playful deeds and jokes."*
>
> —Saint Thomas Aquinas

according to a medieval record, was so holy that he fasted from all food every Friday!). In fact, infants and toddlers can be utterly exasperating, with their spitting up, drooling, fussing, bed wetting, teething, howling, tantrums, and so many countless demands made on already busy parents that sometimes the parents are so worn out that the only time their children seem lovable is when they are sound asleep. (But of course this really isn't the children's fault—it's just proof of how much they depend on their parents, especially when they are very little.)

I think that some of the reasons Jesus loved children so much are because they are genuinely humble, realizing their helplessness and dependence on others, because they are so grateful when they get help, and because they have such awe and enthusiastic appreciation for the beauty of the world God made. Everything seems thrilling to very young children because it is all new and therefore amazing. And not only is the whole world miraculous to young and as yet unspoiled children, but the children themselves are miraculous.

Morning prayers are important because they get each new day off to a good start. "Hello!" "Good morning." Aren't those the most natural and the first things we say when we come into contact with someone for the first time after an absence? So isn't it rather strange that so many people who think they believe that God is real never think of saying those words to him when a new day begins, a day that he has generously made for them? This usually happens because it never occurred to some people to get into the habit of greeting God first thing in the morning. And if the habit wasn't formed very early it becomes harder to start doing it later. Don't be afraid that by teaching your youngsters to say morning prayers you will be imposing an extra burden on them. If they have been doing this ever since they first learned to talk, it will seem to them as obvious and normal to greet God at the start of each new day as it is to speak to you when they wake up.

I once heard about a nun who was so busy that she didn't often have time to spend long hours in prayer, and she shocked many of her sisters by calling out, "Hi, God!" as she ran to her next assignment. This informality seemed irreverent and undignified to some of her pious sisters, but she was simply showing how close she felt to God at all times. She didn't need to be kneeling in a chapel to establish contact with him. Similarly, children shouldn't have to go to church or synagogue to be in contact with their Maker and Best Friend, so quick and informal improvised morning prayers should be encouraged.

At first "Hello!" or "Hi, God!" and something like, "Thanks for yesterday and help today to be just as nice" will be enough. But sometimes yesterday was not a good day and children may feel a need the next morning to complain or to express regrets, praying that this new day will be better. In such a case, they shouldn't lay all the blame on God but think hard about what went

"Children and young people are our greatest treasure. . . . To me children are worth more than all my music. . . . We should say to each of them: Do you know what you are? You are a marvel, a miracle. You are unique. Since the beginning of the world there has not been and until the end of the world there will not be another child exactly like you. "And look at your body— what a wonder it is! Your eyes, your arms, your cunning fingers, the way you move! And when you grow up, can you then harm another who is, like you, a marvel? You must cherish one another. You must work—we all must work— to make this world worthy of its children."

—Pablo Casals

"Pray as if everything depended on God and act as if every-thing depended on oneself."

—Saint Ignatius of Loyola

wrong. Were they perhaps rude to someone so that that person didn't like them, and perhaps did they deserve that, or maybe overreact to criticism? Is there someone they need to forgive or apologize to?

Praying means contacting God and getting his help, but it doesn't mean leaving everything up to him. Prayer is a reminder of how things ought to be ("on earth as it is in heaven") and also of what we ourselves can do to improve our lives, to surmount our misfortunes, and to help other people.

It is extremely important that children learn to supplement their prayers with actions, which prove one's sincerity and therefore speak louder than words. That's why one of the great benefits of morning prayers is that they are forward-looking and reminders to follow up words with good deeds. They set the children's minds on how they should act during the day ahead. They are like preventive medicine.

The influence of morning prayers should not stop when the clock strikes noon. A mother who was teaching her child to swim discovered this one day. She noticed that the girl was taking a big gulp of air and then holding her breath while paddling furiously and getting exhausted, so she told her to keep breathing while she swam, saying that was the way she would be able to make it across the pool. She has described what happened next:

"Be ye doers of the word and not hearers only, deceiving your own selves. . . . By works a person is justified, and not by words alone. . . . As the body without the soul is dead, so faith without works is dead also. . . ."

—The Epistle of James

While watching Beth, I wondered, "Do I treat my prayers like that, relying on one big gulp in the morning to get me through the day?" Beth finally learned to take in breaths as she swam, and I learned to turn my thoughts to God steadily throughout the day. Now we can both go the distance.

—Katherine T. Choi,
in *Guideposts* magazine

"Lift up your heart to Him, sometimes even at your meals... the least little remembrance will always be acceptable to Him. You need not cry very loud. He is nearer to us than we are aware of."

—Brother Lawrence, in
The Practice of the Presence of God

Saying grace at mealtime is another way to remind children to think about God during the day. Mealtime prayers should not be lengthy, or hungry youngsters will get impatient and resent them. But just before breakfast or lunch, tea time or supper, or when rising from the table at the end of the meal, it is polite to thank God for our food, just as we would thank any host or hostess who was giving us a good meal.

There is, however, one important difference. Whenever thanking God for anything we have received, a few thoughts on behalf of other people should be added because loving our neighbors as ourselves is something God wants—in fact, has commanded—us to do. When we forget to include other people in our prayers, the prayers are incomplete.

One custom that many families practice is to hold hands around the table as soon as they sit down together and then say something like, "Thank you, God, for the food we are about to eat, and please give food to other people who are hungry too." It need not always be the parents who say the prayers; children are flattered when they are asked to make up a short grace of their own.

"How much children can teach adults about wonder and simple joys!"

—Fred Rogers of the television program for preschoolers, *Mister Rogers' Neighborhood*

If children sometimes forget to pray or forget to include requests on behalf of other people when they pray for themselves, don't scold them. We all forget things at times, and they can always make up for a lapse sometime later. Remember that one of God's specialties is to forgive.

By far the most vital thing that parents can do for their kids to give them a truly genuine spiritual life is to help them keep hold of that sense of awe that they have when they are young. The world's best artists, poets, philosophers, scientists, doctors, parents, nuns, ministers, and priests never lose this sense of awe of the world, but a great many people do, and this is sad because it impoverishes them.

So here, to close this chapter and to remind us how to make every day a good one, is a reflection about how much one child held on to this wonderful sense of wonder:

One of my favorite comics is Bil Keane's "The Family Circus." In one particular cartoon, Billy's teacher is telling the class, "Today we'll talk about the Seven Wonders of the World." Billy, in his seat, is thinking, "Seven? I thought there were at least seven thousand!" We then see his mental interpretations of the wonders in his world: a long-necked giraffe at the zoo, a bug crawling on the sidewalk, a lovely snowfall, the magic of blowing bubbles with a bubble wand, finding an occupied bird's nest in the fork of a tree, watching cirrus clouds change shape, ad infinitum.

Billy, you see, in the infinite wisdom of a child, is taking time to stop and smell the roses.

—from *My Sunday Visitor*

Part Two

EVENING PRAYERS

"I hear no voice, I feel no touch,
I see no glory bright;
Yet I know that God is near,
In darkness as in light.
He watches ever by my side,
And hears my whispered prayer;
The Father of His little child
Both night and day doth care."

—Evening prayer, *author unknown*

THE "THANK YOU" PART

"Decide to be happy. Render others happy. Proclaim your joy. Love passionately your miraculous life. . . . Do not wait for a better world. Be grateful for every moment of life. Switch on and keep on the positive buttons in yourself, those marked optimism, serenity, confidence, positive thinking. Love, pray, and thank God every day. Meditate—smile—whistle—sing—dance. Look with fascination at everything. Fill your lungs and heart with liberty. Be yourself fully and immensely. . . . Feel God in your body, mind, heart and soul. . . ."

—Robert Muller

Bedtime prayers have a soothing effect. Children like them (although nowadays so many never get a chance to find out that they would) because they help them calm down after they have been over-excited—and most exuberant, healthy youngsters are over-excited by the end of an active day. They need help in winding down. Ordering children to be quiet accomplishes little except to make the children (and the one giving the order) irritable, but giving them something genuinely calming to do—like praying—will make them peaceful.

It is understandable that most of us would be reluctant to teach our children the following traditional bedtime prayer, which was once almost universally used in an era when the death rate among children was very high:

> Now I lay me down to sleep.
> I pray to God my soul to keep.
> If I should die before I wake,
> I pray to God my soul to take.
> If I should live for other days,
> I pray the Lord to guide my ways.

"When you eat a fruit, you must thank the man who has planted the tree."

—Vietnamese proverb

"Our hearts are restless until they rest in Thee."

—Saint Augustine

But today bedtime prayers have become not only less frightening but also less formal. They are usually longer and more leisurely than morning prayers, and most children plunge into them eagerly.

Especially when they are shared with an affectionate, interested parent, evening prayers can provide solid comfort, cozy warmth, and a useful transition between running around wildly and becoming peaceful in preparation for sleep and pleasant dreams.

Once the habit of saying thanks in their evening prayers has been formed, most children will be delighted, because it's fun to recall things that happened during the day that were fun, and thus to prolong and relive them. All a parent may need to do to start them off is to give them a simple cue such as, "Okay, what things do you feel especially thankful for today?"

"The worship most acceptable to God comes from a thankful and cheerful heart."

—Plutarch

Even after the most disappointing, difficult, boring, tiring, or "blah" day, there is almost always *something* to be thankful for, although it may take a bit of searching to remember it. If so, encourage your child to pretend he or she is a detective or a pirate searching for buried treasure.

Even when a sad day has occurred, when someone loved has moved away or died, you can remind your children to be very thankful for having known that person and having enjoyed good times together.

Another way you may be able to teach your children how to notice even very small happiness-producing things is by showing them how to play "the glad game," which was invented by the famous fictional heroine Pollyanna. She was a delightful child with a sense of humor who shared her secret of happiness with everyone she met, even her mean, grouchy aunt, and gradually transformed them by observing and appreciating even the smallest blessings while ignoring their meanness and rudeness. If everybody really tried to do this, imagine how much happier we would be as more and more grouches turned into jolly and kind people.

"The most important prayer in the world is just two words long: 'Thank you.'"

—Meister Eckhart

Of course, playing "the glad game" will not always produce the same happy results it did for Pollyanna, but

> "Life is a mirror; if you frown at it, it frowns back; if you smile, it returns the greeting."
>
> —William Thackeray

we can at least help our children find satisfaction in doing what is right just because it is right, not because they expect people to admire them for it. When they do something good God will see it and be glad, and as long as he and they know about it that should be enough of a reward to make them happy. It can be a secret between the two of them—and children love secrets.

When children learn to take time to notice every day's pleasures and learn to verbalize their happy feelings in their evening prayers, this fosters a warm sharing time, which is a lovely and comforting way to end each day. Cultivating an attitude of gratitude helps develop the sort of consistently cheerful temperament that makes a person able to remain calm even when difficulties arise, pleasant and kind even when other people are cross, patient in a traffic jam, hopeful when everyone else is frightened or gloomy. It helps one add a bit of happiness to the world.

> "All my life I have noticed that outstanding people of every religion have something very special in common. They all seem to be grateful. They possess the fundamental wisdom that we are all children of a gracious God, a God who loves us dearly. God is unchanging love. And our best response to honor His love is gratitude."
>
> —John Catoir

So encourage your children to keep hold of that precious sense of wonder which comes so naturally to them when they are young. It's important to expose children as much as possible to beauty and goodness: through good books and trips to museums and parks. Uttering prayers of thanks can't do the job alone—they need to be supplemented and reinforced by appropriate happiness-producing activities. So keep on helping your children to develop interests and to make good friends, and to be appreciative of everything funny or lovely, nice things they might overlook, little kindnesses that have been shown them, problems that have been solved, and dangers that have been avoided.

"I think we all sin by needlessly disobeying the apostolic injunction to 'rejoice' as much as by anything else."

—C. S. Lewis

THE "SORRY" PART

"A minister asked a class of children, 'If all the good people in the world were red and all the bad people were green, what color would you be?' One little girl frowned and pondered the question. Then her face brightened and she answered, 'I'd be streaky.' This youngster made a point for all of us. Think of yourself as 'good' and you could get complacent. Think of yourself as 'bad' and you could give up any hope of improvement. We all fall short of perfection because we're human. But if we're serious about improving, the Source of all goodness will help us, streaks and all."
—*Christopher Notes*

Unfortunately, on almost every day, most people do something they wish they hadn't done or know they shouldn't have done, or else there is something they have not done that they meant to do. It isn't that we are terrible people, but all of us have faults or imperfections, big or little. Acknowledging this universal fact of life helps to make us realistic and gives us a sense of perspective.

This doesn't mean that children should dwell each day on their worst points, berating themselves fiercely for wickedness, hating themselves, wallowing in shame, embarrassment, despair, and a pervading sense of guilt and hopelessness. It just means that it's a helpful thing to admit—candidly but without exaggeration—that they aren't perfect. This can also remind them to accept the fact that other people aren't perfect either, which should make them more patient, understanding, tolerant, and forgiving. Jesus said we cannot fairly judge others if we ignore the beam in our own eye while complaining about the speck in another person's eye. He also pointed out in the Lord's prayer that our own faults will be forgiven only to the extent that we forgive faults against us.

Checking up on ourselves each day, with a sincere resolution to try not to repeat our mistakes, helps us gradually—slowly but surely, if we keep it up—become better and better people, more likable, more useful, and probably more popular.

Being aware of our shortcomings counteracts any tendency we may have to become smug and conceited. If we don't do that type of daily review we are very apt to repress awareness of real emotional problems. A general and vague sense of guilt, without any

> *"I offer up unto Thee my prayers and intercessions, for those especially who have in any matter hurt, grieved, or found fault with me, or who have done me any damage or displeasure. For all those also whom, at any time, I have vexed, troubled, burdened, and scandalized, by words or deeds, knowingly or in ignorance: that Thou wouldst grant us all equal pardon for our sins, and for our offenses against each other."*
>
> —Thomas à Kempis

> *"Teach me to feel another's woe,*
> *To hide the fault I see;*
> *That mercy I to others show*
> *That mercy show to me."*
>
> —Alexander Pope

clear understanding of what it is we feel guilty about, if unchecked, can escalate into an unjustified, destructive, crippling feeling of worthlessness, lack of self-esteem, and even depression. There are some children who unjustly blame themselves for things that are not their fault at all. For example, when a parent gets sick or dies, they may feel that somehow they did something to cause the disaster. Make sure to reassure your children, if you suspect they might feel this way.

An examination of conscience should be realistic, specific, and brief—and once a failing, even if it is a serious one, has been admitted, the child (and the parent) should no longer dwell on it. After a simple, honest admission of repentance (and if possible, figuring out a way to make up for it), let it go. It's over and should not be brought up again later. Confession clears the air and cleans the soul, and children should feel relieved and happy that they have faced a fault and gotten rid of it.

Also, and this is extremely important, never, ever punish children for a misdeed they have confessed in the privacy of prayer. Never hold it against them or bring it up again later. A child's prayers must be fearless as well as honest, and they

"If we cannot see the central importance to our sanity of recognizing what we are really like in those bouts of self-examination which to a large extent prayer must be, then we are unlikely ever to discover who we are. Worse, with every protraction of our unwillingness to face ourselves as we actually are when we pray. . . our identity slips further and further from us. For the fact is that it is not enough to fall into the conventional language of prayer. There must be some real confrontation with ourselves before there can be any significant lifting of the heart to God. Children do it easily—most children, anyway—until they are taught to overlay and interrupt their colloquies with elegant phrases. . . . Even the most hallowed of approaches to God, hallowed by millions of performances over thousands of days and nights, even they can become a way of deceiving ourselves about ourselves."

—Barry Ulanov

won't be if you use them as a weapon against them. Confession should release people from guilt, so that they don't have to keep carrying the burden of their mistakes and follies over into tomorrow. A person's conscience is sacred territory, so we must not tread on it, or crush it, or we will produce someone who doesn't dare trust other people, who is afraid to open himself or herself up and who therefore shoves his or her conscience aside and ignores it, and you won't like the kind of person you have helped to produce if you let that happen.

> *"Treat people as if they were what they ought to be and you help them become what they are capable of being."*
>
> —Johann Wolfgang von Goethe

Another warning: don't use standardized lists of "sins" if you query children about what, if anything, they may have done wrong today. These may be very inappropriate. It's their own conscience they should be learning to listen to and obey, not anyone else's. There is a story about an eight-year-old boy who startled a priest by confessing that he had committed adultery; he didn't know what the word meant but had seen it in a list of sins, so, being embarrassed to reveal his ignorance by asking what it was, he decided to play safe by admitting it.

And don't put negative thoughts in your child's head either, by asking such questions as "Did you tell any lies?" or "Did you take anything that didn't belong to you?" If you do that you may put unwholesome notions in an innocent head. By and large children act the way they think we expect them to. If they know we take for granted that they will usually behave well, they will almost always do their best to do so, trying to please us. But if they think we are convinced that they are habitually naughty, they may decide they might as well be. So don't be suspicious and ask questions that make it sound as if you expect them to misbehave.

If you really know your own children—and this type of nightly review will help you get to know each other well if you truly use it as a period to drop other activities and to discuss problems with each other—you will learn (and so will they) what particular weaknesses they are prone to such as temper, impatience, selfishness, stubbornness, laziness, discouragement, bossiness, boredom, rudeness, whatever. You can then suggest, very gently, things they should think about and try to correct.

But be very careful always to distinguish between unintentional mistakes and deliberate wrongdoing. Remember that it is unjust and harmful to inculcate children with a sense of guilt where guilt doesn't exist. For example, young children are often clumsy and may accidentally spill milk or break a glass. But this isn't done on purpose (unless it is done in anger), so scolding will just make a child already ashamed and embarrassed feel even worse, convinced he or she is hopelessly inept (and the resulting nervousness will increase the chances of similar future accidents). Instead, sympathize and help the child feel better by suggesting a way to make up for the mishap, such as cleaning up the mess—and then say thanks. And later, if the child brings up the matter during the "sorry" part of prayer, remind him or her that it was just an accident, not a sin, and comfort the

> *"You cannot teach a child to take care of himself, unless you let him try. He will make mistakes, and of these mistakes will come his wisdom."*
>
> —Henry Ward Beecher

> *"Being human we are all liable to err. It is our duty to be understanding and kind towards one who has committed an error and is repentant. . . . Punishment does not purify; if anything it only hardens children."*
>
> —Mahatma Gandhi

49

"If you have behaved badly, repent, make what amends you can and address yourself to the task of behaving better next time. On no account brood over your wrongdoing. Rolling in the muck is not the best way of getting clean."

—Aldous Huxley, in *Brave New World*

child by thanking him or her again for doing such a good job in cleaning up. (I learned to handle such problems in this way by getting the wise advice of Haim Ginott, a wonderful child psychologist, after several episodes in which I had reacted negatively and scolded my increasingly unhappy youngster. I found out how effective the constructive way of handling such situations is—my daughter who had been a nearly hopeless butterfingers was quickly cured.)

Always use the "sorry" part of prayer time to help your children cope with their troubles and learn from their mistakes, not to scold or punish them, which will only have the effect of making them reluctant to admit their wrongdoings to you. Talk things over with them calmly, not angrily. After they have admitted something they may feel a bit ashamed of, you might try asking a question such as, "Why do you think you did that?" or, "Can you think of a better way you could handle something like that next time?" or, "Can you think of anything you could do tomorrow to make up for that?" These types of questions can produce hope for improvement rather than emphasizing defects and defeats. We all would like to like ourselves and to be liked by other people—so your children really want you to help them learn to be "good."

"See everything; praise most things; overlook many things; correct a few things."

—Pope John XXIII

Furthermore, on a day when they say they have done nothing wrong, don't try to get them to search their consciences more deeply. Take their word for it and rejoice with them that it was a great day and that they were great too! You must trust them to tell you the truth if you want them to trust you.

THE "PLEASE HELP" PART

"Do not be anxious about anything, but in everything, by prayer and petition, with thanksgiving, present your requests to God. And the peace of God, which transcends all understanding, will guard your heart and your minds in Christ Jesus."
—Philippians 4:6-7

Petitionary prayer is the most common type of prayer. Many people never pray at all except when they are in need and ask for God's help, hoping he exists and will come to their aid.

So many people in the world are in need of help! Sometimes people we don't know are. Sometimes our friends are. Sometimes we ourselves are. Is there anything we can do about this, other than worry and get depressed?

Yes!

Acquiring the habit of learning to notice and care about people's needs, and having a sincere desire to help them even if we can't think of just how to do so, makes us become more thoughtful and generous than we would be if we were never willing to think about anything unpleasant and never bothered to expand our horizon beyond our own small world. Charity may begin at home, but it shouldn't end there.

> *"Worry never baked a cake, built a bridge, or solved a problem. Fretting does little more than make a bad situation worse."*
>
> —*Christopher Notes*

Asking God for help is beneficial because it increases our realization of how much we all depend on each other, and if we follow through with that thought it can help us think of practical ways in which we ourselves may be able to help others. It is therefore a good idea to have children think for a minute or two every evening about people who are experiencing difficulties, who are suffering. This keeps us real; it keeps religion from being phony or mere sentimentality.

Another reason that asking God's help is valuable is because prayer is an antidote to worry. When we worry we are unhappy and nervous, fearing that the worst is going to happen, but prayer is calming and hopeful.

> *"Worry is interest paid in advance for a debt you may never owe."*
>
> —Anonymous

Although it is true that an all-knowing God does not need to be reminded of anyone's needs, *we* do. As John Kennedy once said, "On this earth God's work must truly be our own," so we should help our children learn to become the kind of people who are both brave and patient in facing their own problems and generous and helpful to other people. God doesn't always remove people's problems, at least not right away, but he supports us through them, teaching us to trust him as we move on and helping us think of some ways in which we ourselves can alleviate or remove them.

"Do not be overcome by evil, but overcome evil with good."

—Romans 12:21

Don't be afraid to talk to your children about the fact that many people in the world are very sick, very poor, very frightened, persecuted, etc. This will give them a realistic awareness that evil exists—and that it should be combated. Almost all children today watch television regularly, and on every news program there are frightful things that we once would have tried to protect them from knowing about. They have seen people mugged, robbed, abused, and killed. They have seen victims of fires, hurricanes, floods, famines, and wars. So you won't be startling them by talking to them about people who suffer from these horrors. On the contrary, by suggesting that you and they pray for such people you will be giving them something constructive to do, thus helping them feel more involved in the struggle against evil.

> "Today somebody is suffering, today somebody is in the street; today somebody is hungry. Our work is for today; yesterday has gone, tomorrow has not yet come. We have only today to make Jesus known, loved, served, fed, clothed, sheltered. Do not wait for tomorrow: tomorrow we will not have them if we do not feed them today."
>
> —Mother Teresa

Not all of us are in a position to be able to perform great works of mercy, but even small ones help. There won't always be big things that children can do for others, but even small acts of kindness are valuable. There are many people, right in our own communities, who are

> "This news is old enough, yet it is every day's news ... there was never yet a philosopher who could endure the toothache patiently."
>
> —William Shakespeare

poor or homeless, whom we can help in many little ways. Just a kind word, a smile, or a little bit of money can have a great impact on others. No gift to help someone is too small if it is given with love.

Keep your children honest, though. It may be sad, but most of us, unlike Mother Teresa, cannot feel the pain of a stranger's hunger or illness as acutely as we feel our own. Something like a child's toothache (or earache or tummy ache) is bound to seem to that child a larger problem than problems of anonymous people in far off places. So if your children are unhappy at school or because So-and-So was mean to them or for some other reason, it won't do any good to tell them not to complain because there are homeless beggars in India who are far worse off than they are.

Of course, it is to be hoped that your children's problems will never be as dreadful as those of people who suffer in war-torn lands or famine-stricken countries, but since their own problems are life-size to them, encourage openness about describing their fears and weaknesses without shame or embarrassment. However, don't *plant* fears by suggesting them (as in the case of one child who told her mother, "I wouldn't have been scared of going to the dentist if you hadn't told me to be brave").

Children will become narrow-minded and selfish if they think *only* about their own problems. They need to think of and to care about their own *and* others' problems if they are to grow into mature and complete human beings. So after you have reminded them to pray for other people, remind them also not to neglect themselves. Assure them

> "The deepest principle in human nature is the craving to be appreciated."
>
> —William James

that you also care about their own personal concerns. Show them you love them and want to listen to their complaints and worries and that you take them seriously. Don't let them think you care more about strangers than you do about them.

They probably won't need any prodding to pray for themselves, but even so a few sympathetic reminders from you might be welcome as proof that you really do care about them and their welfare and to show that you have been listening to them. So you might, for instance, suggest that they remember to ask for God's help with a specific problem they have told you they have. And then, with a hug, you could tell them that in your own bedtime prayers tonight you will be sure to include them and their needs. You can also give them a reassuring thought to go to sleep on by explaining that their current problems are certain to get better.

So far I have been discussing only times when children need help in order to learn how to become better, more generous, people. But there are other important areas where children need even more help, particularly in learning how to forgive. Christ's order that we must love our enemies is extremely hard to understand and accept, both for children and even most adults. When we think someone has wronged us, the anger we feel is normal, yet there is no doubt that

"Let nothing disturb thee. Let nothing dismay thee; all things pass; God alone never changes. Patience attains all that it strives for. One who has God finds he lacks nothing. God alone suffices."

—Saint Teresa of Avila

"Faith can turn trials into triumphs and gloom into gladness."

—Winston Churchill

"I have always believed that God never gives us a cross to bear larger than we can carry. No matter what, He wants us to be happy, not sad. Birds sing after a storm. Why shouldn't we?"

—Rose Kennedy

"If you do not forgive others then the wrongs you have done will not be forgiven by your Father."

—Matthew 6:15

God asks us to forgive. God wants us to have peace on earth, and for this to happen forgiveness is necessary. And difficult as it is to do, it is possible to forgive, even when one has suffered a terrible injustice.

Terry Anderson, an American journalist, was one of many foreigners in Lebanon who were kidnapped and imprisoned by Islamic militants in the 1980s. He was kept in captivity in ghastly conditions—lying in filth, with his feet chained to his bed, often blindfolded and in solitary confinement, with inadequate food, but he managed to keep his sanity by refusing to give in to the temptation to hate his torturers. When he was finally released after nearly seven years of captivity, in December 1991, they sorrowfully apologized for the way they had treated him, and he publicly forgave them and wished them well.

"'Lord, how often am I to forgive my brother if he goes on wronging me? As many as seven times?' Jesus remarked, 'I do not say seven times; I say seventy times seven.'"

—Matthew 18:21-22

Another wonderful example of forgiveness is Steven McDonald, a New York City policeman whose life and that of his family were changed forever when he was shot by a teenage thug. He was completely paralyzed from the neck down and now must spend all his time strapped to a wheelchair with a respirator to enable him to breathe and speak. Instead of staying home feeling justifiably sorry for himself, he has instead regularly visited schools to teach students about the importance of forgiveness and the need for an end to violence. He has even managed to make a trip to Ireland, which he called Project Reconciliation, where "I'll tell my story and try to convince a few maybe to forgive someone."

Before leaving he told reporters, "I never said it is easy to forgive ... but through the grace of God and the prayers of many New Yorkers, I was able to find the strength and faith to forgive the young man who shot me. I have learned that the path of peace and happiness for me has been forgiveness ... in forgiving you come to peace with the world, with all around you." He admits that he wishes he could have survived the shooting "whole bodied" so that he could play ball with his son (who was born soon after the accident) "and be able to put my arms around him." But he also says, "I believe that God has designs for all of us" and "I pray all the time ... and I've asked him to make me an instrument of his peace."

A couple who have studied the subject of forgiveness and taught it to children explain what is involved:

> The Greek word for forgiveness actually means "let go of" ... ideally, someone who has wronged us feels regret and is willing to make restitution. But many offenders don't choose to do so and... the hard truth is, whether they do penance or not, the one who pays the price for our own unforgiveness is us, not the other person. ... Forgiving ultimately means giving up the investment in staying angry and taking vengeance by returning abuse directly or indirectly, e.g., continually badmouthing the other person. Forgiveness is complete when the memory of the incident no longer carries an emotional charge. ... Forgiveness is needed [when] someone is holding on to anger or hurt. ... Forgiveness cleans

> *"He who cannot forgive others breaks the bridge over which he must pass himself."*
>
> —Anonymous

> *"Forgiveness is the answer to the child's dream of a miracle by which that which was broken is made whole again, what is soiled is again made clean."*
>
> —Dag Hammarskjöld, in *Markings*

57

the slate so that both people can "win," both people can communicate afresh. That's not possible where vengeance and withholding remain available options.

—Jacqui Bishop and Mary Grute, R.N.

"Write injuries in dust, benefits in marble."

—Benjamin Franklin

But of course, important as it obviously is to forgive others, this doesn't mean that it isn't very hard to do when someone has hurt us badly. So let a little time go by for the wound to at least partially heal before expecting most children to be capable of forgiving. And be careful—if you ask your children if perhaps they did something to cause the incident, or emphasize the duty to forgive too soon, your children may think you are on the other person's side and you too will seem to become an enemy. They may stop trusting and confiding in you. So sympathize with them saying you understand why they are so angry. Only after you have convinced them that you are definitely on their side whether they are right or wrong should you remind them that in either case they must learn how and why to forgive, for their own sake.

"When I forgive my enemy have I not turned my enemy into my friend?"

—Abraham Lincoln

For a while children may be angry at God as well as at their "enemies" for having allowed a situation to happen, but it is okay for them to admit this.

"The only people with whom you should try to get even are those who have helped you."

—John E. Southard

It can be especially hard for children to forgive if they are certain that what another person did to them was terribly wrong. It seems unfair to let someone off the hook instead of seeing to it that he or she gets punished when children are sure they were right and the other person was wrong. But there are always two sides to any story, and we can explain that perhaps both of them were partly wrong and partly right.

In the end, however, it is most important that children forgive themselves as well as their "enemies."

"God Himself does not propose to judge a man until he is dead. So why should I?"

—Samuel Johnson

"If you judge people, you have no time to love them."

—Mother Teresa

THE "GOD BLESS" PART

"The Lord bless you and keep you; the Lord make his face to shine upon you, and be gracious to you; the Lord lift up his countenance upon you, and give you peace."

—Numbers 6:24

To keep a balanced and wholesome perspective toward prayer it is a good idea not to overdo contrition or requests for help, but after a few moments to turn our thoughts in a different direction, with a kind of open-ended lovingness—no longer thinking so much about ourselves and stressing apologies or problems, but just pausing to think about all the good things and people in this world that we love and would like to bless.

With an unsleepy, sociable, imaginative, and resourceful child, the "God bless" part of prayer has a tendency to s-t-r-e-t-c-h. Alan Funt, on his TV program

"Praise God from whom all blessings flow."

—Thomas Ken

"Little boy kneels at the foot of the bed,
Droops on the little hands little gold head.
Hush! Hush! Whisper who dares!
Christopher Robin is saying his prayers.
God bless Mummy, I know that's right. . . .
Oh! God bless Daddy —
I quite forgot. . . .
Thank you, God, for a lovely day.
And what was the other I had to say?
I said 'bless Daddy,' so what can it be?
Oh! Now I remember it. God bless me. . . ."

—from "Vespers,"
a poem by A. A. Milne

Candid Camera, once recorded the bedtime prayers of a child who managed to extend the "God bless" part to so many people and things that it took twenty minutes.

You may begin to feel rather hard-hearted, wanting to cut this part of evening prayers shorter than your children want it to be, sounding as if you don't like it when your children are so loving and want to wish such an enormous number of people well. But this is nothing to feel guilty about. Instead, remind them that there will be a tomorrow. Explain that you're sorry that you have leave now but that they are free to continue—by themselves—to think of more and more people and things to bless, ad infinitum, until they fall asleep. What better way could there be to fall asleep than to do so by blessing everybody in the world? It definitely beats counting sheep.

So although you don't want to cut them short, don't let them use this part of nightly prayers as a con game to postpone "lights out" and your departure indefinitely. Don't, in other words, let them become selfish while deluding themselves into thinking they are being unselfish.

This part of prayer will help to give you insight into their likes and dislikes, priorities and values. Don't try to lead or inhibit them, but let them be completely natural and sincere. The small as well as big things in their lives that they appreciate will come into view, and no doubt some things you may not consider nearly as wonderful as they do, like soda pop, hamburgers, candy, chewing gum, and violent TV. Let them name them. And if you feel like laughing in disbelief or snorting in disgust at some of their favorite things, try to refrain.

That is, of course, unless they are blessing with affection something really tasteless or dangerous, in which case carefully explain to them the problem. If you criticize their taste too frequently or with too much annoyance they may return the annoyance and both of you will get upset. You may damage the relationship you have with them or even their relationship with God.

But don't expect prayer to do all the work in molding a child's character. Prayers must be supplemented with other activities as a follow-through. Outside of prayer times you will have many chances to guide their tastes by exposing them to people you admire and to worthwhile things that you value and want them to learn to appreciate. You might want to take special trips to cultural events that the children could enjoy such as special concerts, children's theaters, art exhibits, science museums, and libraries.

Some of the excuses usually given for not taking part in activities such as these are that "my children are bored by such things" or "they

*"He prayeth best
who loveth best
All things both great
and small,
For the dear God who
loveth us,
He made and loveth all."*

—Samuel Taylor
Coleridge

*"I see the moon,
And the moon sees me;
God bless the moon,
And God bless me."*

—Celtic child's saying

*"Dear Father:
hear and bless
Thy beasts and
singing birds,
And guard with
tenderness
Small things that have
no words."*

—Anonymous

*"Love all God's creation,
both the whole and every
grain of sand. Love every
leaf, every ray of light.
Love the animals, love the
plants, love every separate
thing. If you love each of
these, then you will become
aware of the mystery of
God in all; and when you
do, you will thereafter grow
every day into a further
understanding of it."*

—Fyodor Dostoyevsky,
in *The Brothers
Karamazov*

squirm and chatter during shows or exhibits so much that it's embarrassing and annoying to other people," which sounds very much like the explanations given by parents who give up on teaching their children to pray, as described in the introduction to this book.

Parents need to explain to young children how they should behave when we introduce them to prayer and, similarly, when introducing them to any new experience. If we carefully explain how much they will enjoy these things once they behave attentively they will become curious and receptive. So ease into new experiences gradually, at first taking them on a very short trip to an interesting museum or art exhibit, staying only briefly so that they don't get tired— and soon they will enjoy themselves and want more. And then they will be able to add these new happy experiences to all the other wonderful things they want to bless.

In the end, though, it is important to remind your children to pray for even things and people they don't like. You can talk to them about how *everyone* benefits from blessings. Explain that the word "blessed" is a synonym for "happy," so the more we bless others the happier we and they should feel.

Remind your children that if they bear a grudge against someone they dislike they will be hurting themselves because it will embitter them, and bitterness will keep them unhappy. It might also cause them to be unjust to someone. Therefore, although their natural instinct will be to focus on people and things they love, at least some of those they bless should be non-favorites. Asking God's blessing on people we don't like is similar to loving our enemies, which Jesus told us to do. Thus, by doing that, we will become more truly generous and loving people.

"God bless Mother and Daddy, my brother and sister, and God, do take care of Yourself because if anything happens to You we're all sunk."

—a little boy's prayer quoted by President George Bush

"Let us love one another, because love is from God. . . . Everyone who loves is a child of God and knows God."

—I John 4:7

Part Three

OCCASIONS FOR SHORT, SPONTANEOUS PRAYERS

"Some visitors to Calcutta asked me to tell them something that would be useful for them to lead lives in a more profitable way. I answered, 'Smile at each other. Smile at your children, at all. Let mutual love for others grow each day in all of you. . . . Peace starts with a smile.'"

—Mother Teresa

> *"I tell you, whoever does not accept the kingdom of God like a child will never enter it.' And He put his arms around them, laid his hands upon them, and blessed them."*
>
> —Mark 10:15

Although morning, mealtime, and bedtime prayers are all useful when bringing up children, it is important, especially in the beginning before the habit of praying has become well established, to go easy. Children are not contemplative monks or nuns who are willing or eager to spend many hours a day in formal prayer. The biblical injunction to "pray always" isn't appealing or even comprehensible to small children, and if we overdo our demands we will cause resentment.

Yet there are many additional, unexpected times when spontaneous little prayers are almost instinctive to them. For example, when children fall down and hurt themselves, especially if they are really injured badly or are bleeding, although their first response may be to scream, "Ouch! Mean old floor!" their second instinct may be to beg God to help them by taking away the pain. And if they don't think right away of doing that, you can give them the idea by saying aloud for them something like, "Please, God, we really need your help right now!"

When God allows unpleasant things to happen to us, it reminds me of the times when a mother has upset her children by scolding them or denying them something they asked for. They need comfort, but the only person with them to whom they can turn for comfort is their mother. So, still sobbing, they climb up on her lap and she puts her arms around them and hugs them. It's the same way with God: we need to turn to him for comfort when we are deeply troubled, even if we are inclined to blame him for the trouble. And strange as it seems, turning to him does bring us comfort.

Just as we may spontaneously turn to him when we need help, we should also turn to him when others need help. I think it encourages generosity if you suggest that whenever your children see an ambulance or a fire engine they should say a brief prayer for the people who are ill or injured. My children developed this practice as a habit, and it made them happy to think they were doing something, even though just a very small thing, to help these people who needed help. In fact, their concern for strangers in need grew into something that put me to shame.

I remember vividly one day when my young son and I were walking home from school and we noticed a man, apparently unconscious, lying on the pavement in the school playground. We couldn't tell if he had been hurt or was drunk or sick. I kept on walking, but my son stopped me and asked, "Aren't you going to see what's the matter with that man? He may need help." I said it was none of my business, and he replied indignantly, "If you don't do something to help that man I'll never believe in God again!" This was a challenge I didn't dare ignore, so I went over to the man and investigated. To my relief I found that he wasn't injured but was just resting— but this taught me who the Good Samaritan in my family was, and I recalled Jesus' warning about how we must become like little children if we want to go to heaven. So when we teach our children to know, love, and obey God we should realize that sometimes they teach us more than we teach them.

"Is not Jesus pointing to children even as models for grownups?"

—Pope John Paul II

I used to love going on leisurely walks around our neighborhood with my youngsters because they had such eager curiosity about everything they saw. They smiled at every passerby, patted every dog on a leash, peered into every mailbox and automobile and shop window and garage and courtyard garden, admired every tree and flower, and made me feel as if all of these had been put there for our personal pleasure.

Our strolls produced some interesting experiences. One day, for example, when I was pushing my little girl in her stroller, an elderly drunk came weaving toward her and said, woozily, "God bless you, darlin'. And have a good life because [sighing] you only have one." He then wobbled away and Katie called out to him saying, "God bless you too!" He turned and smiled at her again and then, gallantly tipping his hat, said, "Thank you, dearie," and blew her a kiss before disappearing. Then on the next block, we saw another man, also obviously inebriated. This one was slumped on a doorstep. Katie was singing lustily at the top of her lungs, and he glared at her and snarled, "Shut up, kid! Your noise is giving me a headache. Besides, what's there to be so damn happy about?" Instead of being hurt or angry, Katie said under her breath, "That poor man. He's so cranky. Please help him, God."

The two men reminded me of the two thieves, the "good thief" and the other one, on the crosses next to Jesus during the crucifixion, because in both cases the men's situations were the same but their responses were so different. This shows how often our good or bad fate is not ordained by God but is our own responsibility. We create our own good or bad "luck" or "fate" through our positive or negative attitudes, depending on how we choose to make use of our wonderful God-given free will, for better or worse.

My other point in telling these anecdotes is to emphasize that even impromptu prayers of just two or three

> *"So long as one does not become simple like a child, one does not get divine illumination. Forget all the worldly knowledge you have acquired and become like a child, and then you will receive the divine wisdom."*
>
> —Hindu teacher Ramakrishna

words, or even no words at all, just a kind thought or, as Mother Teresa said, a loving smile, can be as genuine a prayer as a lengthy formal one. What God wants from us is love for our neighbors, including strangers (though of course with young children always under adult supervision), and my children have shown me that it doesn't require a lot of words to express that. The great British philosopher Bertrand Russell said it well:

> *"God is love; he who dwells in love is dwelling in God, and God in him."*
>
> —I John 4:I

> The root of the matter is a very simple and old-fashioned thing, a thing so simple that I am almost ashamed to mention it for fear of the derisive smile with which wise cynics will greet my words. The thing I mean—please forgive me for mentioning it—is love, Christian love, or compassion.

Part Four

CHILDREN'S PRAYERS
AROUND THE WORLD

"All the world's religions are similar because they help us to become better human beings. . . . Human beings naturally possess different interests. So it is not surprising that we have many different religious traditions with different ways of thinking and behaving. But this variety is a way for everyone to be happy . . . Because the important point of all the different religious traditions is to be helpful, we must maintain harmony and respect between them. This will benefit not only the followers of each religion, but will make our own neighborhoods and countries more peaceful. To do this we need to understand something about the world's different religions . . . the more we understand of each other's ways, the more we can learn from each other. And the more easily we can develop respect and tolerance in our own lives and in our behavior towards each other. This will certainly help to increase peace and friendship throughout the world, which is one of the aims of all major religions."

—The Dalai Lama

In addition to the unexpected times when children may say short impromptu individual prayers, there are many social occasions involving prayer that they can look forward to observing with their families. These include both secular holidays and specifically religious holy days. The word "holiday" is derived from holy day, so even a recreational occasion which seemingly has no religious aspect actually does have a connection with religion.

Prayers are appropriate on secular occasions observed all over the world, such as birthdays, anniversaries, national holidays, Mother's Day, Father's Day, and in some countries Children's Day, Grandmothers' Day, and Teacher's Day. In addition to these there are a great many special religious observances in which children participate.

Buddhist children celebrate the birthday of Buddha in different ways in different countries. In Japan's cities processions of thousands of children march to Buddhist temples carrying lotus blossoms. A statue of the child Buddha stands in each temple in a flowery shrine near a metal basin filled with tea, and the children give their flowers to the statue and then pour the tea over it. In Cambodia, Laos, Sri Lanka, Thailand, and Vietnam, Buddha's birth, enlightenment, and death are all celebrated together during the full moon of the year's sixth lunar month because the people believe that all three events occurred on the night of the full moon. In Laos, although the morning is devoted to religious solemnities, the afternoon is a time for recreation, with a rocket festival and parades of dancers and musicians entertaining everyone.

> "Children are the same the world over ... Customs and traditions and background may be different. Some children may be shy and withdrawn, others aggressive, some may be unhappy and hungry and diseased, but they all respond to the same treatment. They all respond to one lovely little four letter word — love."
>
> —Danny Kaye

In Thailand, Buddhists believe that no boy will ever be fully mature unless he spends some time as a monk. When this time comes, a final meal is held at home for the boys chosen to spend the next three months in a monastery. The boys are given special dishes but are not allowed to speak at the meal. After it is over the boys' heads and eyebrows are shaved, and the next morning they are led in a procession bright with banners and flags to the monastery where they will spend their time serving the monks, praying, and studying Buddhist teachings.

Hindu children and adults honor many gods. Although Hindus seem to outsiders to be polytheistic, they actually are not. They believe in one Creator, Brahma, and all the other "gods" are merely aspects or reincarnations ("avatars") of him. Some of these are special favorites of children. For instance, they celebrate the birthday of Rama, the seventh incarnation of the major god Vishnu and the hero of the *Ramayana*, one of India's greatest epics, by painting their classrooms and themselves and guests with colored powders and giving out garlands of flowers. Teej is another popular festival in honor of the god Siva and his wife Parvati and is observed with parades and plays. And the birthday of Krishna, the eighth incarnation of Vishnu and the most beloved of all the gods to many Indian children because he is so approachable, and as a child was so playful and mischievous, is observed enthusiastically with games, storytelling, dancing, music, and Krishna's favorite foods.

In addition to these celebrations there are special Hindu family ceremonies held in honor of children: to welcome newborns and to name them; to honor brothers and sisters; and to celebrate boys' birthdays, until Upanayanam, "The Beginning of Wisdom," on their eleventh, twelfth, or thirteenth birthday (the age depends on which caste they belong to) when they receive their "Second Birth" and become adults.

Jewish children observe the Sabbath with their families every week on Saturday as a day of rest and prayer. (We owe thanks for our weekends to Jews and Moslems who refused to work on Saturdays and Sundays.) Jews also observe Rosh Hashanah (the first day of the Jewish New Year) and ten days later Yom Kippur (the Day of Atonement). Both of these are high holy days marked by meditation on life and death. Another important observance is Pentecost (the Feast of Weeks), commemorating the anniversary of the revelation of the Ten Commandments to Moses.

One of the days that is a favorite of Jewish children is Simbat Torah ("Rejoicing in the Law"), which is observed with parades of children marching around synagogues waving flags. Another is Purim, a joyous festival that commemorates the rescue of Jews from a massacre through the courageous intervention of the beautiful Queen Esther. When a parent reads aloud this story from scripture, the children often stamp their feet and hiss every time the villains are mentioned and cheer loudly at every mention of Esther.

The seven days of Passover are an especially important time. They commemorate the Exodus of the Jews from slavery in Egypt, and on the first evening there is a ceremonial supper called a Seder at which the youngest child present plays an important role.

In the autumn there is a "Feast of Tabernacles," which lasts for seven or eight days. It originated in agricultural communities as a time to thank God for a good harvest and got its name from the temporary shelters that were used by workers in the fields. But today, even in some cities, it is observed especially by families with children who construct straw huts that they cover with flowers and use for picnics and even for sleepovers on clear nights.

In December, the special festival of Hanukkah arrives. This eight-day Festival of Lights commemorates a miracle believed to have occurred in the year 165 B.C. when the Maccabees, a group of Jews fighting against persecution, gained control of their temple in Jerusalem, but found that it contained only one day's supply of holy oil. Yet, amazingly, the oil lasted for eight days until a new supply arrived. In memory of this, Jewish families light eight candles in succession, one each evening, on a candelabrum called a "menorah," and each evening there are special foods, prayers, stories, and presents for the children. The evenings are also traditional times for games such as cards, chess, and a favorite of the children played with a four-sided spinning top invented in medieval Germany called a "dreidel."

But perhaps the greatest day in a Jewish child's life is the day when childhood ends: the Bar or Bat Mitzvah, when boys and girls come of age on their thirteenth birthday. To get ready for this big day they have studied the Torah and prepared a speech they will deliver to the assembled families and friends, from whom they will receive gifts on this day.

Moslem children get a special treat on Ashura, the ninth day of the first month of Islam's year, on which they commemorate the safe landing of Noah's Ark. According to their tradition, Noah's wife celebrated the ending of the flood by making for her family a sweet pudding filled with nuts and fruits; her recipe has been handed down and this pudding is still eaten on this day. But the most joyful day of the Moslem year is Mohammed's birthday, celebrated all over the world with parades, visits to families and friends, gifts of food to the poor, and readings of scripture. Incidentally, Mohammed loved and enjoyed children so much that he often said his prayers while letting his little grandson ride piggyback on his shoulders.

The most solemn time of the year for Moslems is Ramadan, the ninth month, during which everyone except children and the very old may not eat, drink, or smoke from dawn to twilight. Although children are exempt from fasting they observe the month in two ways: they go from house to house singing special songs in praise of those who fast and are rewarded by receiving handfuls of nuts and sweets, and they study scripture and take part in a big celebration called Khatma when they have read all 114 chapters of the Koran for the first time. Their parents then proudly take them to friends' houses and at each one they read some verses and receive congratulations, sweets, and other presents. Their teachers also receive gifts at this time, to thank them for their work with the children. At the end of Ramadan cannons and drums announce that the fast is over and three days of celebration begin during which the children receive gifts, including new clothes, and usually a fair is held with magicians and jugglers, music, a miniature circus, fireworks, and camels and elephants to ride.

"Jesus loves the little children, All the children of the world, Red and yellow, black and white, They are precious in his sight. . ."

—Author unknown

Christian children, too, enjoy a large number of days on which to celebrate, and the entire next chapter will describe how these are observed throughout the year.

Although these different religious traditions vary greatly in many ways, they also have a lot in common. Periods of penance are important in Buddhism, Islam, Judaism, and Christianity, and the Jewish Bar Mitzvah resembles the Hindu boy's Second Birth. Although some of the customs may seem strange to people in other cultures, they all evolved in response to universal spiritual needs. Now, in these days when ease of transportation and communication has ended the isolation of people on different continents, it is more important than ever to teach our children (and ourselves) to respect other cultures.

Part Five

CHRISTIAN HOLIDAYS AND OTHER SPECIAL DAYS THROUGHOUT THE YEAR

"Let us come into His presence with thanksgiving; let us make a joyful noise to Him with songs of praise."

—Psalm 95:2

January 1 is the day most people throughout the world celebrate New Year's Day. It is the start of a new calendar year and often a time to set new goals or to begin something new. To give young children a special treat on New Year's Eve, let them stay up late enough to watch television and see the new year arrive in different countries at different times around the world. This will be a geography lesson they will actually enjoy.

Norwegian children have observed January 5 with a mixture of ancient pagan, Christian, and secular celebrations known as Julebukk ("Yule Buck") ever since the time when the Vikings worshiped the god Thor and his pet goat and went from house to house carrying goats' heads or stars on top of poles, singing folk songs and hymns, and being welcomed with gifts of sweets or money. But in 1966 generous Norwegian Boy Scouts and Girl Guides transformed the day by placing UNICEF posters on top of their poles and carrying leaflets about its work on behalf of needy children, along with empty milk cartons in which they asked people to place donations for UNICEF instead of giving them personal treats.

January 6, or the Sunday between the second and the eighth day of the month, is observed by Christians as Epiphany, or Twelfth Night, or the Feast of the Three Kings, in memory of the night when the Kings or Magi (meaning "Wise Men") arrived in Bethlehem and brought gifts to the infant Jesus. In some countries this, rather than Christmas, is when families exchange gifts. In Italy there is an ancient legend that says that when the Magi were searching for Jesus they invited an old woman named Befana (her name is an abbreviation of Epiphany) to join them, but she was busy sweeping her floors so she didn't go with them. Later she tried to find the Christ Child by herself, but she never succeeded, so she still searches for him every year on this evening, flying around on her broomstick, visiting every home and leaving presents for all good children.

January 13 is Saint Knut's Day, a holiday in Denmark, Norway, and Sweden, named for King Knut (or Canute) who ruled Scandinavia in the eleventh century. He decreed that the festive Yuletide season should last for twenty days. Parties are held on this, the final, day, and in Sweden it is called Yule Plundertime, when decorations are removed from Christmas trees, with children eating up the cookie ornaments and then tossing the trees out the window.

January 17 is San Antonio's Day in Latin America. Saint Anthony (along with Saint Francis of Assisi) is known as a protector of animals, so in many countries youngsters take their pets and other animals to church to be blessed and sprinkled with holy water on this day, hoping to protect them against accidents and disease during the coming year. In Mexico, children dress up their pets for the occasion. Cows and donkeys, painted with stripes and polka dots, crowd the streets, along with rabbits wearing bonnets, parrots with neckties, and hens, chickens, dogs, and cats wearing dresses and coats.

In Bulgaria, January 20 is Grandmothers' Day. The children visit their grandmothers, as well as the midwives or doctors and nurses who helped bring them into the world, and give them bouquets of flowers.

In Ireland, February 1 is the Feast Day of Saint Brigid. Brigid means "bride," and the Irish call her "sweet Saint Bride of the yellow, yellow hair." She was renowned for her beauty as well as for her charity and many miracles, reputed to cure the sick and insane, heal lepers, and give sight to the blind. Born a slave, she was later influential in abolishing slavery in Ireland. She spent her childhood and much of her adult life—even though she became a nun and founded many monasteries—as a dairymaid and is now a patron saint of Ireland and of people in the dairy industry. Children can relate to her fondly because she was known for falling asleep during Saint Patrick's long sermons.

February 12 is the Feast of Our Lady of Lourdes. It commemorates the visions that Saint Bernadette, a French peasant girl, saw of the Virgin Mary in Lourdes in 1850. Ever since then the shrine built at Lourdes has been a unique source of healing, and each year it is visited by more than four million people, not only ill people hoping to be cured but great numbers of kind volunteers who give up their free time to take care of the sick and disabled.

February 14 is Saint Valentine's Day when people think of those they love, and it is often celebrated with greeting cards, flowers, candy, and other gifts. Many school children make cards that they send unsigned to their classmates, with phrases like, "Be my Valentine. I love you. Guess who!" But it can be a sad and embarrassing day for children who don't receive any Valentines, so encourage your children to be kind by giving cards to all their classmates instead of just their favorites.

February 29 is Leap Year Day. This is celebrated only once every four years, because under the Gregorian calendar now used by most countries the year consists of 365 days, but it actually takes that many days plus five hours, forty minutes, and forty-five seconds for the earth to create a year by revolving around the sun, so one more day is added to the year every four years. Children born on February 29 get a chance to celebrate their birthdays only once every four years, so parents try to make it an extra special day for them.

March 21 is a national holiday in Mexico. It is the Day of the Indian Child, celebrating the birthday of Benito Juarez, Mexico's first president who was a full-blooded Indian. On this day exhibits are held of paintings and handicrafts made by Indian children.

In February, March, and April, the penitential season of Lent is observed for forty days before Easter, in memory of the forty days Jesus spent in meditation in the desert to prepare for his public life. The dates of Lent vary depending on the date of Easter, which is a movable feast occurring each year on the Sunday after the first full moon following the spring equinox.

In previous centuries Lent was observed very strictly, so it became customary in France, Germany, Greece, Spain, and Latin America for people to take advantage of their last chance to enjoy themselves before the days of penance began. On the last Saturday before Lent, a special carnival exclusively for children is held in Trinidad and Tobago. Children prepare for this day for weeks, joining masque bands (groups that choose themes from fairy tales or other popular stories) and making costumes. When Saturday arrives, they hold parades and sing and dance dressed in their costumes, and bands compete for prizes. In Latin America, Carnival (the word means "without meat"), on the Tuesday before Lent, is the major holiday of the year.

The first day of Lent is Ash Wednesday, so named because priests make the sign of the cross with ashes on churchgoers' foreheads to remind them that "you are dust and unto dust you shall return" or to "repent and believe the Good News." Many people will not wash the ashes from their foreheads, but rather wear them thoughtfully until they finally fade away.

The austerities of Lent are relaxed on March 17, Saint Patrick's Day. Along with church services and parties, this day features big parades with bands of school children marching and twirling batons and waving small green silk or paper flags. Irish people and their friends in other lands dress up in green and wear shamrocks, the little three-leafed plants that Saint Patrick used to illustrate how the Holy Trinity of God the Father, Jesus the Son, and the

Holy Spirit are three distinct but equal persons united in one God.

The name "Lent" comes from the Anglo Saxon word "lencten" referring to the lengthening of the days at this time of year. It seems fitting that Easter arrives right after the spring equinox when nature itself experiences a resurrection.

In the eighth century, Venerable Bede, an English monk and historian, speculated that the word "Easter" may have come from "Eostre," the Anglo Saxon name of a Teutonic goddess of spring and fertility whose symbol was a rabbit—which may explain the origin of the Easter bunny. And eggs may have become a special Easter symbol of rebirth because for many centuries they were among the foods forbidden during Lent. Today coloring and decorating Easter eggs and taking part in egg hunts and races in which eggs are rolled with spoons are very popular Easter traditions among children.

"Join, then, all of you,
Join in our Master's
rejoicing.
Rich men and poor men,
Sing and dance together.
You that have fasted
And you that have not,
Make merry today.
Christ is risen:
The world below is in ruins.
Christ is risen:
The spirits of evil are fallen.
The angels of God
are rejoicing."

—Hippolytus,
235 A.D.

Because Easter commemorates the resurrection of Christ and his triumph over death, it is the most joyous day of the Christian year. But three days before Easter arrives comes Good Friday, the saddest day of the year, remembering when Christ was betrayed by one of his disciples and then tortured and executed as a common criminal.

Willard Hunter, a distinguished columnist on politics and religion, wrote a thought-provoking article about Good Friday asking why we call it good:

Good Friday, when God reportedly gave up his own son, is called "Good" because the tragedy of that day resulted in renaissance throughout the world. In the words of George Clarke Peck's famous essay, "All the armies that ever marched, all the navies that ever sailed, all the parliaments that ever sat, and all the kings and presidents that ever governed, put together, have not affected life as it is lived on this planet as much as has that One Solitary Life. ..."

On Good Friday, some communities will be giving the people an opportunity to observe the anniversary of Christ's death by means of an outdoor Way of the Cross. Others will sit quietly in churches. For all, the day will provide opportunities to consider how the bad is often transfigured into the good—how Good Friday's tragedy becomes Easter Sunday's liberation.

Fifty days after Easter is Pentecost. This is a holy day for both Jews and Christians. For Jews it commemorates the establishment of their eternal covenant with God; for Christians it commemorates the descent of the Holy Spirit upon the Apostles, inspiring them to go forth and preach the gospel, and is thus considered the birthday of the church.

"Our Lord has written the promise of Resurrection not in books but in every leaf of springtime."

—Martin Luther

In April, the first day of the month is April Fool's Day when children enjoy playing pranks on people. As long as the pranks are amusing and harmless, this is a wonderful opportunity to celebrate having a sense of humor and to enjoy a little fun.

In April and May, three countries observe a Children's Day. In Turkey, on April 23, students elected by their classmates are given free transportation to national and local government offices to observe how government works. They enjoy ice cream and movies, and visiting foreign children are also invited to participate in parades and parties. In Japan, the fifth of May used to be observed as Boys' Day when all families that had a son flew a kite in the shape of a carp over their house. The carp was chosen, as a symbol of traits parents wanted their sons to have, because of its strength and courage when it swims upstream. However, since 1945 the day has become one on which girls are honored as well as boys. The children go to Shinto shrines where priests bless them, and afterward families enjoy a special meal together. In Nigeria, schools are closed on Children's Day, May 27. Special radio and television programs are broadcast, and prayers are offered in mosques and churches. The day also includes movies, dances, sports events, and exhibitions of children's art.

The month of May is consecrated in many countries to the Virgin Mary, and in France on May 1 it is customary for young girls to wear corsages of white flowers in her honor.

On the second Sunday in May, Mother's Day is observed in the United States. This day is also observed all over the world, but on many different dates. On this day, children honor their mothers and give them cards, flowers, and other gifts.

May 30 is the church's official feast day of Joan of Arc, the brave teenage girl who helped end the English invasion of France in 1429 and who was then burned alive for being a witch (for wearing boys' clothing among other things). She was declared innocent seventeen years after her death and is now a patron saint of France. She is so beloved by the French that they are not content to celebrate her life on just one day; the people in Orleans hold celebrations in her honor on May 6, the anniversary of the day when "the Maid of Orleans" liberated their city, and celebrations in the rest of France are held on May 2.

The month of June is when fathers get thanked on Father's Day. Children make some small gift for their dads and hug them just as they did for their moms the month before on Mother's Day. Good fathers remind us of our Father in heaven, and we should show both of them gratitude for helping to take care of us.

The month of July brings with it, on the fourth, Independence Day in the United States, with displays of fireworks (*not* in our homes where they are both illegal and dangerous). But forbidding children's fireworks need not diminish the day's pleasures, which include picnics and parades, and almost all communities put on displays of legal fireworks far more beautiful and thrilling than any that amateurs could produce. So let your children stay up late to see these. This is also a day to teach American youngsters about their heritage: "one nation under God indivisible with liberty and justice for all." On this day it's a good idea to take children to church and to pray that everyone might enjoy the right to freedom and happiness that is the goal of the Declaration of Independence.

> "Of all the habits that lead to political prosperity, religion and morality are indispensable supports. In vain would men claim the tributes of patriotism who would work to destroy these great pillars of human happiness."
>
> —George Washington

On August 6, people in Paraguay celebrate the Day of the Child with puppet shows, games, dances, and songs. The country's Girl Guides stage publicity campaigns in connection with the day to make people more aware of the needs of children.

In September, Labor Day starts off the month in America as the last gasp of summer and is quickly followed by "back to school." Children for whom the opening day of school is their first step into the outside world may be very anxious and will need to be encouraged to look forward to it as an exciting adventure rather than as something to be feared, and as a wonderful chance for them to make many new friends.

"Live your life by the Golden Rule. It's really not hard to do. Just remember to treat all others as you would have them treat you."

—Author unknown

Most children will be glad to go back to school as they look forward to seeing their friends again, but some may be nervous because they have had difficulty keeping up with the class work or because a few kids in school are bullies. Here is a beautiful prayer by Saint Francis de Sales that you might quote for them or that they might even want to memorize:

Have no fear for what tomorrow may bring. The same loving God who cares for you today will take care of you tomorrow and every day. God will either shield you from suffering or give you unfailing strength to bear it. Be at peace then, and put aside all anxious thoughts and imaginings.

In October, a beautiful month in the northern hemisphere when the trees are aflame with red and golden leaves, the thirteenth is a national holiday in Portugal. It commemorates the final vision of Our Lady seen by three young children who were severely punished for lying when they told their parents about the visions and persecuted by government officials when they maintained their story. But the children courageously returned six times to the spot where they claimed this had happened, and the final vision was so spectacular that it at last convinced 10,000 eyewitnesses as well as cynical journalists that all the visions were genuine. Our Lady of Fatima became the patron saint of Portugal.

The last day of October is one that children especially love: Halloween. For the Christian church this was originally known as All Hallow's Eve, the eve of All Saints' Day when the faithful venerate all believers who have died, especially those who have no feast days of their own. Gradually, thinking about the dead at this time of year gave way to dressing up in costumes resembling skeletons or ghosts or even devils, and the night became a time for children to act devilishly. The custom of "Trick or Treat" ("Give me a treat or I'll play a trick on you") also began.

Then, in 1950, the evening again became associated with religion when Reverend Clyde M. Alison of the Presbyterian Church in Bridesburg, Pennsylvania, persuaded his Sunday school class to help poor children by going out on Halloween and collecting money for UNICEF, the United Nations Children's Fund, instead of candy for themselves. They did and raised $17, and this modest beginning inspired so many other children that by 1965 over three million children in more than 13,000 communities in the U.S. and Canada were "trick or treating" for UNICEF and raised $2,000,000. Halloween had once again become concerned with death, but now it was a time to work to prevent it. Ambassador Hambre of Norway made a speech at the United Nations saying that UNICEF's gifts to "all the healthy, happy and robust children in the world" are as valuable as the help it gives to underprivileged children because it helps the more fortunate ones to "learn the joy of giving" by teaching them "the profound importance of personal contributions" and of "good deeds." In 1957 President Lyndon Johnson proclaimed October 31 as National UNICEF Day.

In October and November in the United States and Canada, the biggest day for families is Thanksgiving Day. It is observed in Canada on the second Monday in October and in the U.S. on the fourth Thursday of November. Most Americans assume that the day was started by the Pilgrims in Plymouth, Massachusetts, in 1621, but actually there were several Thanksgivings celebrated before that. Sir Francis Drake held one near San Francisco in 1579, and one was held in Virginia in 1614. Elements of the day can also be found in ancient harvest festivals in Europe. But it is the one held by the Pilgrims that captured the imagination of Americans. Held in gratitude for a successful harvest, they shared it with neighboring Indians who had befriended them, taught them how to survive in the wilderness, and introduced them to new foods and crops such as turkey, cranberries, corn (maize), and pumpkins. It is still customary to eat these foods on this day. Although Thanksgiving has become in many homes a time to overeat, it is important to remember its religious purpose of giving thanks to God for our food. We would do well to say grace at every meal, but especially before this very special one.

December is an especially joyous time for Christian children and adults as the Christmas season begins.

The season of Advent, a month-long period of preparation, starts things off. The word "advent" means "coming," and the purpose of this period is to prepare with reverence and eagerness for Jesus' coming. Many families make it festive, setting an Advent wreath of pine needles and holly with four tall candles on a table. On the first Sunday of Advent one candle is lit, two on the next Sunday, and so on until all four candles are lit. On Christmas Eve, the wreath is replaced with a single candle, called a "Christ candle." Children are given Advent calendars, which contain numbered doors for every day of the month to be opened to reveal special pictures of winter activities, with a picture of the Holy Family around the manger behind the door for Christmas Eve.

December 6 is Saint Nicholas Day. In the fourth century Bishop Nicholas of Myra, in what is now Turkey, once took pity on three girls in a poor family and secretly threw a bag containing gold through their bedroom window on three successive nights. Afterward the grateful girls learned who had done this, and ever since then his name has been associated with gift giving.

> *"There seems a magic in the very name of Christmas. Petty jealousies and discords are forgotten ... Would that Christmas lasted the whole year through."*
>
> —Charles Dickens

In Holland he is nicknamed "Sinteklaas" and arrives a week before his feast day, dressed in a bishop's robes. Church bells greet him, and he rides through towns on a white horse leading parades with brass bands and cheering children. This sets off a whole week of preparations for his feast day. On Christmas Eve he leaves switches for naughty children but gingerbread cookies and chocolate letters with their initials on them for all good children.

In Venezuela Saint Nicholas rides on his white horse to visit schools, hospitals, and orphanages where he hands out toys and sweets.

In America, where he is known as Santa Claus, he is no longer depicted as a dignified bishop but as a jolly, stout fellow in a red suit who lives at the North Pole and travels around the world on Christmas Eve carrying large bags bulging with toys, riding through the sky in a sleigh pulled by reindeer, and climbing down chimneys to deliver his gifts. This surprising transformation in the image of Saint Nicholas is the result of a poem written in 1823 by Clement Moore, an Episcopal minister who was trying to amuse one of his children who was seriously ill. He was embarrassed when friends who enjoyed the poem had it published, but it received immediate and undying popularity.

Some people think it is wrong to let little children believe in Santa Claus because later, when they learn he is imaginary, they might be disillusioned and no longer trust their parents' word. But one of the most famous editorials ever written, published annually at Christmastime in the *New York Sun* for fifty-two years until the paper ceased publication, ardently defended the myth. It was written by Francis P. Church in response to a query by an eight-year-old girl named Virginia O'Hanlon. She had written to the newspaper saying some of her little friends had told her there is no Santa. Here are excerpts from his editorial:

> Virginia, your little friends are wrong. They have been affected by the skepticism of a skeptical age. They do not believe except they see. . . .

> Yes, Virginia, there is a Santa Claus. He exists as certainly as love and generosity and devotion exist, and you know that they abound and give your life its highest beauty and joy. Alas! how dreary would be the world if there were no Santa Claus! It would be as dreary as if there were no Virginias. There would be no childlike faith then, no poetry, no romance to make tolerable this existence. . . .

> The most real things in the world are those that neither children nor men can see. ... Nobody can conceive or imagine all the wonders there are unseen and unseeable in the world. . . .

> Is it all real? Ah, Virginia, in all this world there is nothing else real and abiding.

> No Santa Claus! Thank God! he lives and lives forever. A thousand years from now... he will continue to make glad the heart of childhood.

In Austria, Germany, and Switzerland, Christmas trees are decorated on Christmas Eve, but children are not allowed to help. They stay outside the room, excitedly waiting for the door to open when they will find out what Kris Kringle has brought them. But in other countries Christmas Eve is usually the night when families decorate their trees together and children hang up stockings that parents or Saint Nicholas or Santa Claus or, in England, Father Christmas will fill with gifts during the night. Many families attend church services in the early evening or at midnight, and in some churches children dress up as shepherds and angels and surround a Christmas crib.

Nobody knows the exact date of Christ's birth, but in the fourth century the church decided to observe it around the time of the winter solstice, on December 25, replacing an ancient Roman winter festival called the Saturnalia which started on December 17 and ended on "Natalis Solis Invicti" (the Day of the Birth of the Unconquered Sun) when people exchanged greetings and gifts and rejoiced that the darkest days of the year were over. So the birthday of the sun was transformed into the birthday of the Son of God.

On December 26 the first Christian martyr, Saint Stephen, was stoned to death. One of his persecutors that day was Saul of Tarsus, a zealous Jew who hated Christians until he had a miraculous conversion, hearing the risen Christ ask him, "Saul, Saul, why do you persecute

"May the Christ Child bring you enough happiness to keep you sweet, enough trials to keep you strong, enough sorrow to keep you human, enough failure to keep you humble, enough success to keep you eager, enough friends to give you comfort, enough wealth to meet your needs, enough enthusiasm to look forward, enough faith to banish depression, enough determination to make each day better than yesterday, enough love to exclude no one and to embrace everyone, enough generosity to become God's gift to others, enough spiritual vision to attain fulfillment in becoming other 'Christs.'"

—Author unknown

me?" After that conversion he became Saint Paul, one of the greatest of the apostles, converting and guiding many Gentiles until he, too, was finally martyred. It was certainly not easy or safe to be a Christian in those days, but the blood of the heroic martyrs became the seeds of the future church.

The twenty-eighth of December is the Feast of the Holy Innocents on which people honor the infants who were murdered by King Herod's soldiers when Herod wanted to make sure that the newborn child Jesus was killed. He didn't succeed in having Jesus killed, however, thanks to a prophetic dream Saint Joseph had, warning him of the plot, and the Holy Family escaped to Egypt before the killings began. The feast in honor of the infants who died in place of Jesus is the last feast day of the Christian year.

Part Six

HELPING CHILDREN WHO
HAVE DOUBTS

"Do not believe every spirit, but test them to see whether or not they are of God, for many false prophets have gone out into the world ... Love one another, for love is from God; and every one who loves is born of God, and knows God. Someone who does not love does not know God, because God is love ... No one has ever seen God, but if we love one another God dwells in us ... We love him because he first loved us."

—The Gospel of John

Small children may at times have a few complaints and doubts about God, as expressed in the following examples from Eric Marshall and Stuart Hample's collection of children's letters to God:

> Why can't you even keep it from raining on Saturday all the time?
> Rose

> Dear God,
> My friend Arthur says you make all the flowers. I don't believe it.
> Best wishes,
> Benjamin

> Dear God,
> Are you real? Some people don't believe it. If you are you better do something quick.
> Harriet Ann

By the time children go off to elementary school, where in most cases in the United States no prayer or even mention of God is allowed (in fact, not long ago a teacher was actually fired for leading her pupils in prayer after one of them had died), they begin to meet a great many people who don't believe in God. In many cases, these people are so caught up in the materialistic culture we live in that they have never given any thought to religion. Our children are then exposed almost daily to so many influences different from those of their own family that parents who believe in God may find it very difficult to

"God does not die on the day when we cease to believe in a personal deity; but we die on the day when our lives cease to be illuminated by the steady radiance renewed daily, of a wonder the source of which is beyond all reason."

—Dag Hammarskjöld

continue to pass their own faith and values along to their children. It now becomes more important than ever to supervise their morning and evening prayers and to share with them the religious holidays and feasts you know they enjoy, so that they will continue to have a close relationship with God.

It is not really surprising that many children will start to have more serious doubts about God when they begin meeting many people who don't believe in him. Children who have been taught to pray may begin to feel embarrassed if they are teased about it, and start to think that their parents must be weird. And when that happens they might be strongly tempted to rebel against what they have previously enjoyed and found comforting. What can parents do about this? We must rise to the occasion aggressively but also carefully.

"The less I pray, the harder it gets; the more I pray the better it goes."

—Martin Luther

It's important to sound more sympathetic to your children than critical and negative, or your children will think you're nagging and probably stop listening to you. It's far better to praise whatever you can about their behavior or their taste than to focus on criticizing their bad taste. Ever since Adam and Eve people have been tempted by forbidden fruit, so if you tell them they can't go somewhere or play with someone they will probably want to. It's still the way it was with Tom Sawyer who was strictly forbidden to play with Huckleberry Finn, so he therefore played with him whenever he got a chance.

"If criticism did any good the skunk would be extinct by now."

—Fred Allen

So instead of making a blacklist of things and people you don't want your kids to see, focus enthusiastically on things you do want them to see and do. The best way to wean them from dangerous friendships is to encourage good ones. Invite nice children to your home for a meal, or include them on trips to a museum or a good movie or puppet show or a baseball game, or even for overnight visits. Or throw a party on a special occasion and make sure they will enjoy it by letting them pick their favorite foods and by helping you with festive decorations.

Another thing we must do at this time is to take our children's questions and doubts seriously, with respect. They are now starting to ask far more difficult questions—both personal and theological—than when they were little.

Among their personal questions may be these:

"Why do my parents believe in prayer when my classmates' parents don't?"

"My classmates call me a 'goody goody.' Won't they think I'm strange if I keep trying to talk to and listen to God?"

"Why should I turn the other cheek when the nasty bully in our playground hits me, since it just makes him laugh and hit me even harder?"

Among the theological questions about which they may be seriously troubled there will probably be the following. First, there is the most basic one of all: "How can I actually know for sure if there really is such a thing as God when so many people don't think there is?" Second, "If God is real and powerful and loving, then why does he let evil exist? Why are millions of refugees homeless victims of cruel wars? Why does he let

"For a painting to exist, there must be a painter; for a meal to exist, there must be a cook; for a creation to exist, there must be a creator."

—Frank Sheed

so many people, even innocent children, starve to death in famines?" And third, "How do we really know if there is an afterlife? And if there is a heaven and a hell, will I go to hell if I stop praying?"

Unfortunately, simple answers that might have satisfied very young children will no longer work as our children get older and the questions become more complex.

Biblical language can be hard to understand, particularly for children (which is why we need ministers, priests, rabbis, and theologians, who spend their lives studying scripture, to explain its mysteries to us). But the Bible has some wonderful stories that can help us understand who we are and where we came from.

Once upon a time, even before time itself existed, there was nothing. But now zillions of things and people exist. How come? What could have brought about such a tremendous change? What started it all? Something had to be there to set everything else in motion, something with unique and enormous power. Whatever that was had to be the very first "thing," the Creative Force that made everything else that exists possible. In English we call this "thing" "God." And because nothing can produce or give anything to others that it itself does not possess (like an inkwell can give out ink but not milk, for instance), God must possess intelligence, love, and even a sense of humor to create people with these qualities. And since the universe and its inhabitants are obviously real, doesn't this mean that God is also real?

> *In the beginning, God created heaven and earth. ... The earth was without form and empty, with darkness over the face of the deep, and the Spirit of God swept over the surface of the waters. And God said, "Let there be light,"and there was light. And God saw the light, that it was good, and he divided the light from the darkness, and called the light day and the darkness night. And they were the first day.*
>
> —Genesis 1:1-5

The *Origin of Species* by Charles Darwin published in 1859 described how his studies of plants and animals had led him to believe that natural selection and evolution are the process through which creatures develop, and his theory became so widely accepted that in many people's minds it replaced belief in a personal Creator. This was an unwarranted conclusion, however, because it merely describes a process by which creation may take place but says nothing about whether or not a Creator uses this method. In fact, all science can ever explain is the way things operate, but never why they exist. That question is beyond its powers of observation.

> *"The power that created the poodle, the platypus, and people has an integrated sense of both comedy and tragedy."*
>
> —James Thurber

Some scientists think life was created just by accident, but many others think such an idea is ridiculous. How could a mere accident produce a cosmos in which comets circle the earth at incredible speeds on reliable schedules for centuries? The vastness and predictability and complexity of the many elements in the universe have led many great scientists—Sir Arthur Stanley Eddington (an astronomer), Albert Einstein (a physicist), Galileo Galilei (a mathematician and astronomer), Blaise Pascal (a mathematician and philosopher), Louis Pasteur (a chemist), and many, many others—to conclude that an intelligent and very powerful Being created the universe and is in charge of it.

> *"To stand on one's legs and prove God's existence is a very different thing from going on one's knees and thanking him."*
>
> —Søren Kierkegaard

The following statement by a Greek historian who was a pupil of Socrates attests to the fact that most people in every era have believed in some kind of God:

Do you perceive that the wisest and most perdurable of human institutions are ever the most God-fearing; and in the individual man the riper his age and judgment, the deeper his religiousness?

—Xenophon (430-355 B.C.)

The next big question, then, is: "What is God like? Why should we think that the First Cause of everything is a God who cares about individual human beings?"

Although it is true that we cannot fathom the mystery of God completely, we can understand some things about him by analyzing his creation and understanding what is necessary in order to be creative. Hatred is unable to create anything; on the contrary it is destructive. And indifference never created anything either. The only thing that is creative is Love! An artist creates a sculpture or a painting out of love, a husband and wife create a child out of their mutual love.

This means that our Creator must be Love, as it says in the Bible. But if so, there remains that very puzzling and distressing question: "Why does God allow evil to exist, making so many innocent people suffer?" This is "the problem of evil" which has caused many good people to lose their faith in God.

> *"A small boy in Sunday school described how powerful God is; God is more powerful than Batman, Superman, and the Lone Ranger put together."*
>
> —Dick Van Dyke

> *"Thou asketh what God is? I answer shortly to thee: such a one so great is He that no one other is or ever will be of like kind... If thou wilt know properly to speak what God is, I say thou shalt never find an answer to this question... If thou knew what God is thou shouldest be as wise as God... It is enough for thee to know that God exists."*
>
> —Richard Rolle

> *"The reason why the element of paradox comes into all religious thought and statement is because God cannot be comprehended in any human words or in any of the categories of our finite thought."*
>
> —D. M. Baille

Instead of letting children think it is always sinful to doubt God's existence or goodness, we should ponder these questions ourselves. Reading the Book of Job and studying writings of profound thinkers who have grappled with these questions will help.

One answer to explain why God permits evil is that he gave people free will because he considers our freedom more important than forcing us to be good. He wants us to be loving, but love isn't genuine unless it is voluntary. A lot of the injustices that occur in the world are the result of someone's ignorance or willful defiance of God and others. Wars and persecutions exist because too many people hate instead of loving one another.

Many things God has made for us are pleasant, helpful, and necessary even if they sometimes result in tragedies. If God abolished the law of gravity, nobody would ever fall down and hurt themselves, but also there would be nothing to hold us to the earth. If God abolished fire, no one would ever get burned, but we wouldn't be able to cook or be kept warm. If God abolished the wind, there would be no destructive hurricanes, but also no lovely fresh air to breathe. If God abolished water, no one would ever drown, but we would also never be able to drink or bathe or swim. And if God never allowed use to make any mistakes, we would remain ignorant all our lives, because it is through learning from them that we mature.

It is our hope that the tragedies and injustices that have occurred in our present lives will be compensated for in the next one. In the Sermon on the Mount Jesus said:

Blessed are they that mourn, for they shall be comforted. ... Blessed are they who are persecuted ... for theirs is the kingdom of heaven... rejoice and be exceeding glad, for great is your reward in heaven. ...

—Matthew 5:3-12

Of course whether this is true or not depends on our answer to another question: "How do we know there is an afterlife?" Let's look at the example of the butterfly, which for centuries has been depicted in Christian art as a symbol of Christ's resurrection. An unattractive earthbound worm enters its cocoon for a deathlike sleep—and then bursts forth from its "tomb" beautifully transformed and free to fly.

> *"I believe that the suffering we now endure bear no comparison with the splendor, as yet unrevealed, which is in store for us."*
>
> —Romans 8:18

Furthermore, Christianity isn't the only religion that teaches that there is an afterlife. All the world's major religions do. Baha'is compare our present life to that of a baby inside the womb who has no idea how wonderful its life will be after it has emerged from the womb into a much bigger and more fascinating world. Buddhists believe in a continuous cycle of rebirths and that our next life will be better or worse depending on how we behave in this one, until we have finally acquired enough goodness to reach Nirvana, their conception of heaven. Hindus say, "He becomes immortal who seeks the general good of man." Islam teaches that "those who have believed and done things which are right, these shall be inmates of Paradise." Judaism teaches that "the dust returns to the earth as it was, and the Spirit returns to God who gave it." Shinto, a Japanese religion, says, "regard Heaven as your father, Earth as your mother, all things as brothers and sisters, and you will

> *"Love makes people believe in immortality because there seems not to be enough in life for so great a tenderness and it is inconceivable that the most masterful of our emotions should have no more than the spare moments of a few brief years."*
>
> —Robert Louis Stevenson

enjoy the divine country which excels all others." The Sikhs ask, "Why weep when a man dies, since he is only going home?"

The biggest problem for children about immortality is not whether or not there is a heaven but whether there is also a hell. Some children can become very upset if they think they have been naughty enough to go there. When your children forget to say their prayers or stop saying any for a while, or if they have been rude or mean to someone, assure them that if they are sorry such faults are not significant enough to get them there. Hell is only a place for people who hate God and are *extremely* evil. Some theologians even believe that hell exists but is probably empty because nobody is so incurably wicked and unrepentant that they deserve dreadful eternal punishment.

So one thing we must not do about our children's doubts is give in to despair. Even if they rebel against God completely this may be only temporary. Augustine of Hippo was hostile to religion for years before being converted and becoming one of the greatest saints in history. And the author of the popular hymn "Amazing Grace" was a cruel slave trader before he learned to know the loving and forgiving God "who saved a wretch like me." Relax. And enlist God as an ally to help you. He will help. His love for children is so great that he is always eager to bless and embrace them.

> *"To believe with certainty we must begin with doubting."*
>
> —Good King Wenceslaus of Bohemia

Proverbs 22:6 says, "Start a child on the right path and even in old age he will not depart from it." This proverb may have been true in earlier times, but in today's complex society, where there are so many more competing ideologies and temptations, "it ain't necessarily so." Many parents who try hard to lead their children on "the right path" discover that some of them choose different paths. Some docile children accept without any questions whatever they are taught about God, but this may not mean that they are more virtuous than others, simply that they aren't interested enough to be curious. Doubting isn't always a bad thing.

One of the main reasons some people have doubts about God is because of unpleasant traits they associate with him, such as dogmatism, puritanism, and judgment. And if that is why some children discard religion I dare say I think it's sensible of them! The concept of God that children acquire is largely built upon the examples they see of authority figures, so if parents or teachers are uncharitable, harsh, rigid, intolerant, judgmental, or unfair, the children influenced by them will almost surely be inclined to think of God that way—and who could love a God like that? Being told that he is Love will seem hypocritical to them.

"What is important is striking a healthy balance between belief and doubt. When doubt so predominates our life that we become aimless, withdrawn, and self-centered, we need to pray earnestly for faith. When belief so predominates our life that we become self-righteous and dogmatic we need to risk doubting. . . . Realize that there are no shortcuts to spiritual health. Our culture's emphasis on instant gratification has carried over into every aspect of our lives, even the spiritual [but] there is no fast road to faith. Grace requires more of us than a weekly visit to church and impatient prayer. In spiritual matters, patience, persistence, and sincerity are our greatest allies."

—Philip L. Berman

So it is understandable that some children turn away from religion, and therefore instead of feeling horrified if ours do we would be wise to sympathize with them while trying to correct false notions that may have disillusioned them, and to help them realize that God should not be confused with the worst examples of his followers. Therefore, let them follow their own path. Show how pleased you are when they do something you admire, but be patient and tactfully overlook the rest. Just continue to show them you love them. Relax, and leave their future to Providence.

Acquiring a mature faith does not mean that we will ever in this lifetime have answers to all our questions, but that need not trouble us. Saint Augustine once saw a child on a beach taking water from the ocean with a spoon and putting it into his pail. Augustine asked him what he was doing and the boy replied, "I'm trying to collect all this water in my pail." Augustine smiled and said, "But don't you realize that the ocean is too big to fit into your pail?" And then he thought to himself, "But isn't that what I'm trying to do when I try to fit God into my brain?"

Although limitations in our knowledge are inevitable, our knowledge is ultimately not as important as other things, as Saint Paul pointed out in his first letter to the Corinthians:

"Believe that life is worth living and your belief will help create the fact."

—William James, in
The Will to Believe

I may speak in tongues of men or of angels, but if I am without love, I am a sounding brass or a tinkling cymbal. I may have enough faith to move mountains, but if I have no love, I am nothing. And though I give all my goods to the poor but have no love, it profits me nothing.

Love is patient; love is kind and not envious. Love is not boastful; or rude; never selfish or quick to take offense… Love endures all things. It never fails, but prophecies will cease and knowledge will vanish because we now know only in part. But when that which is perfect has come, then that which is only in part shall be taken away.

When I was a child, I spoke as a child, I understood as a child, I thought as a child, but when I became an adult, I put away childish things. And now we only see through a glass, darkly, but later we shall see face to face … and then we shall know even as we are known.

In the meantime, there exist three things that last: faith, hope and love, these three; but the greatest of these is love.

Therefore,
Love life.
Love yourself.
Love your family.
Love the whole world.
Love God.

If you and your children do these five things, you and they are guaranteed happiness, by being constantly aware of and awed by the unspeakable privilege it is to be alive for a while. Prayers of thanksgiving will keep you alert to all the tremendous beauty and variety that exists in the world around us. So notice it. Admire it. Enjoy it. Relish it. Be glad that it and you exist. And use it, adding your own loving contributions to it, thus making our world an even better,

"I don't know what your destiny will be, but I know the only ones among you who will be really happy are those who will have understood how to serve others."

—Albert Schweitzer

happier and more beautiful place than it would be without you!

> "Every time I hear a
> newborn baby cry,
> Or touch a leaf,
> or see the sky,
> Then I know why
> I believe."
>
> —from "I Believe,"
> performed by
> Perry Como

SOME RECOMMENDED BOOKS ABOUT RELIGION FOR YOUNG CHILDREN

Children's Favorite Bible Stories. 256 pages in hardcover, illustrated in color by Delia Halverson and with "A Note for Parents" before each story. Time-Life Books, 1997.

The Family Book of Bible Fun, by Randy Peterson. A 328-page paperback illustrated in black and white, with quizzes and interactive games based on Bible stories. Tyndale House Publishers, Inc., 1994.

Fifty Fabulous Parties for Kids, by Linda Hetzer. A 176-page paperback book illustrated in black and white by Meg Hartigan, with a special section on celebrating holidays, religious events, and other family events. Carol Paperbacks, 1994.

The Golden Children's Bible. 510 pages in hardcover with attractive and realistic color illustrations on almost every page. Golden Books, 1996.

The One Year Book of Devotions for Kids, edited by
Debbe Bible. A large paperback book with a full
page devoted to each day of the year and short biblical quotations and suggestions on how a child can
apply them. Tyndale Publishers, Inc., 1993.

The Rhyme Bible, by Linda J. Sattgast and illustrated
in color by Toni Goffe. 448 pages in hardcover,
with amusing drawings and short poems that para-
phrase the words of the Bible accurately but in a
simple vocabulary. Each verse faces a picture on the
opposite page and accurately and wittily describes
the event illustrated. Multnomah Publishers, 1996.

SOME RECOMMENDED BOOKS FOR PARENTS

Between Heaven and Earth: Prayers and Reflections That Celebrate an Intimate God, by Ken Gire. An unusual book of prayers because of the way it is organized under common questions people ask: What is prayer? Who prays? Why and how do we pray? What struggles do we encounter when we pray? What difference does prayer make in our lives? Harper San Francisco, 1997.

How Do You Spell God? Answers to the Big Questions From Around the World, by Rabbi Marc Gellman and Monsignor Thomas Hartman. This wise and witty book was ostensibly written for teenagers but will appeal to all ages and people of all faiths. The authors worked with Buddhists, Catholics, Hindus, Jews, Moslems, Protestants, and other believers, and this book respectfully explains how we differ but also how much we have in common and is an important guide in teaching understanding and tolerance. Morrow Junior Books, 1995.

How to Make the World a Better Place: 116 Ways You Can Make a Difference, edited by Jeffrey Hollender and Linda Catling. The book gives practical suggestions on how you can help effect positive social change in areas such as the environment, homelessness, hunger, and human rights—with simple actions taking only a few minutes a day. Norton, 1995.

The Pummeled Heart: Finding Peace Though Pain, by Antoinette Bosco. This is a remarkable account of how a devout, brave, and forgiving woman struggled to confront many forms of suffering, including the tragic murder of her son. She offers a magnificent example of how trust and hope and love of God can help us understand why a loving God permits evil to exist but helps give us the strength to overcome it. Anyone who is experiencing pain or sorrow, or whose faith in a God who loves us has weakened because of the existence of evil, should read this important and inspiring book. Twenty-Third Publications, 1994.

Raising Kids Who Care: About Themselves, About Their World, About Each Other, by Kathleen O'Connell Chesto. This book for parents has three sections: an introduction, part one on "Growing Morality," and part two on "Moral Issues Facing Today's Children." Beautifully written by a mother who deplores the self-centeredness so common today, even in prayer which she says is often just an exercise in self-improvement, "me and my relationship with God." She points out that a true relationship with God exists only as part of a relationship with others. And she says family life is where we acquire the ability to see another's need as greater than our own. Just as young children depend on parents to provide for their physical needs they also depend on parents for the emotional and psychological support that will enable them to grow into ethical, caring adults. The satisfaction and pleasure that come from placing the needs of someone you love before your own are the real family values, she says, but today she thinks children are being deprived because society fails to teach the value of self-sacrifice. Sheed and Ward, 1996.

A Scientific Approach to Biblical Mysteries, by Robert W. Faid. The result of fifteen years of research in archeology, history, linguistics, and mathematics, this interesting book presents new evidence that will strengthen the faith of believers and change the minds of people who think the Bible is mostly myth by explaining how some miraculous events can be scientifically authenticated. New Leaf Press, 1993.

Teaching Your Children Values, by Linda and Richard Eyre. The authors of this book have nine children, so they surely should know what they're talking about! Their splendid book provides subjects and methods ranging from those appropriate for preschoolers and elementary school through adolescence. The values included are honesty, courage, peaceability, self-reliance, self-discipline, moderation, fidelity, chastity, loyalty, dependability, respect, love, unselfishness, sensitivity, kindliness, friendliness, justice, and mercy. They come down hard on the "permissive parenting" of the 1960s which they blame for producing a generation of adults who have broken all records for drug abuse, family instability, and suicide. One reason, they say, is that many parents have avoided teaching about values "until the children are old enough to choose their own value system." This, they say, is a "catastrophic mistake," because children have already picked up consciously or subconsciously their own values during their preschool years. The most helpful and original aspect of the book is the teaching methods described. For preschoolers they say the most effective methods are simple games, short stories, and a great deal of praise and reinforcement. With children in elementary school, awards are particularly effective, as are songs and games that require more thought. The quizzes and games suggested are extremely imaginative and are sure to make teaching your children values fun for both you and them. Simon & Schuster, 1993.

INDEX OF QUOTATIONS

Joan Bel Geddes is the author of numerous books on subjects from childcare to the civil rights movement. Her articles have appeared in many magazines and newsletters. Her most recent work is *Childhood and Children: A Compendium of Customs, Theories, Profiles, and Facts* (Oryx Press.) She continues her freelance writing from her home in New York City.